Passion, Plants and Patronage

Passion, Plants and Patronage

300 Years of the Bute Family Landscapes

Kristina Taylor and Robert Peel

Artifice
books on architecture

Contents

Preface

Passion, Plants and Patronage references the passion of the Bute family over the generations. The same energy imbues the research and text undertaken by Robert Peel and Kristina Taylor, and their considerable achievement in bringing a multi-faceted project to fruition.

The joy of reading the text is in the authors' contextualisation of a personal family history within social, political, scientific and cultural history. The momentum of personal projects, and the dialogue between artists, designers, technicians, architects and family members are beautifully described and weave a cohesive and compelling tapestry.

The Bute family have been significant patrons of art, architecture and the landscaped environment over six centuries. Reference points and motifs are repeated throughout the collections, and the built and natural architecture. The direction of one generation's interest to the next was sometimes changed; further initiatives were picked up, and past projects subsequently rekindled. A long term inherent vision has emerged through the process of this momentum.

The current generation were mainly raised at Mount Stuart on the island of Bute, and it was there following the death in 1993 of our father John, 6th Marquess of Bute, that Johnny Bute, Anthony Crichton Stuart and myself returned to the tradition of continuing project work and restoration and commissioning new artwork, landscape and architecture.

Mount Stuart Trust was formed in 1989 to preserve the house, gardens and estate for the future. When the house and gardens were opened to the public in 1995, it was our intention to present an extraordinarily magical context in an innovative fashion. This involved moving outside the box of a standstill historical location and keeping Mount Stuart vibrant and accessible to a contemporary audience.

Nothing stands still—long term planning in terms of planting is ongoing and underpins the landscape of the formal and rural environment. Restoration work continues—much of the decorative work undertaken by Tom Errington during the 1980s and 1990s and subsequent restoration work by Colleen Donaldson and Clare Meredith in 2000 progressed work started by the 3rd Marquess and has been respectively re-interpreted and invigorated by our father, Johnny, Anthony and myself. The contemporary visitor centre opened in 2001 together with the first year of the Visual Arts Programme, and encapsulates in many ways our vision for continuing the tradition of collaboration and dialogue with contemporary thinking and works of excellence.

I have referred mainly to Mount Stuart from familiarity. *Passion, Plants and Patronage* covers the wide range of landscapes developed by the Bute family. The book answers many questions and at the same time sets up exciting lines of enquiry for future research. The text therefore achieves a great deal in linking the various existing archives and developing projects at Cardiff, Luton Hoo and Dumfries House, a trajectory bringing the past, present and future brightly into focus.

Sophie Crichton Stuart, Director of Mount Stuart Trust,
July 2012

Introduction

Whilst studying at the Architectural Association in London on the conservation of landscapes and gardens the Bute family appeared in the history of several of the landscapes about which I was reading. Bute is a name that resonates particularly in Cardiff, where I lived beside Bute Park. Cardiff Castle, Caerphilly Castle, Castell Coch and their settings together with the urban fabric of Cardiff itself owed much to that family.

On wishing to pursue these strands further, the synergy of working with a former fellow student from the Architectural Association seemed inspirational. Kristina's Scottish upbringing led her to follow with particular partiality the Butes' influence in Scotland. We discovered that it was mainly two representatives of the family, the 3rd Earl and the 3rd Marquess, who had commissioned so much in so many places within the British Isles. No systematic study, however, had yet been undertaken. We then began a complex and rewarding detective story to unravel how these landscapes were connected with each other and how they had developed over three centuries, culminating in our book. The support of John Bute, the 7th Marquess, allowing us to consult the archives at Mount Stuart, still being prepared for public access, made the project possible. It helped us reveal an intriguing world of social and artistic connections through the generations and the repetition of certain design motifs, which reflected the particular interests of individual members of the family.

Passion, a quality running through the Bute genes, appears in every generation. In whatever they are interested they tend to commit from the heart. The book title is inspired by the 3rd Earl, who was compulsive in his collecting. Moreover he patronised with a passion, in both a financial and advisory capacity, many with creative talent like the architects Robert Adam and William Chambers, who credited him within his lifetime, and the painters Charles Steuart and George Ehret. A legacy of this is the portfolio of plans of Kew by William Chambers, the Adam brothers' works, the wonderful series of landscape paintings by Steuart of Bute's several properties and the thousands of flower paintings and drawings, many now appropriately housed at The Royal Botanic Gardens, Kew.

His passion for collecting new plants, welcomed into Britain from origins around the world in the eighteenth century, was the force driving the development of Kew Gardens. His influence in their development is perhaps less well known, and is why we have included a chapter on Kew to document the 3rd Earl's involvement and attribute him due worth.

Such consideration is not to belittle the patronage of his descendants. The 3rd Marquess was as passionate about restoring buildings as the 3rd Earl in collecting. He too patronised the arts. William Burges, Robert Weir Schultz and William Goscombe John owe their careers to his initial support and sponsorship. Andrew Pettigrew was employed by him at Dumfries House before becoming gardener at Cardiff Castle and achieving glorious distinction there. Alexander Roos as estate architect has left his particular style on several landscapes owned by the 3rd Marquess.

All the landscapes in the book are now open to the public except Old Place at Mochrum, a much loved family home and well run private estate. Mount Stuart, the family seat of the Butes, is a romantic place. The ferry crossing to the island is an exciting prelude to visiting an astonishing house set on a terrace of land before it drops towards the waters of the Firth of Clyde. The lushness of its garden planting and grandeur of its estate trees can be explored after passing through the elegant modern visitor centre and receiving an interpretation of the visual pleasures ahead. A programme of contemporary art installations enhances part of the garden where the house can act both as backdrop and viewing platform. Falkland House and Palace form part of an integral landscape, which recall important phases of Scottish history while demonstrating the philosophy and special interests of the 3rd Marquess of Bute.

Dumfries House was acquired in 2007 by a consortium of charities and heritage bodies headed by HRH The Prince of Wales in recognition of the special nature of the Adam-designed house, its contents and adjoining land. The several estate buildings are respected for their fine architecture and contribution to the landscape. Some will be used for education purposes and others for teaching traditional crafts and skills as part of an employment scheme. The house and parts of the estate are now open to visitors so that a circuit can be walked and the various unfolding sequence of landscapes enjoyed and appreciated.

Bute Park in Cardiff is undergoing a significant restoration project, supported by the Heritage Lottery Fund, to enhance the landscape and its interpretation and provide for the greater comfort of its visitors. Restoration of park buildings, the conversion of the walled garden into an education and training centre as well as for refreshments, and better signing of its arboretum are included. One new refreshment building is inspired by the wooden summer house attributed to William Burges, which was erected close to the castle but is now at St Fagan's Natural History Museum outside Cardiff. Significantly, there are plans to re-open the north gate of the castle to link it directly with the park as in the time of the Butes, and fill much of the moat with water once again.

Kew, the globally important Royal Botanical Garden and World Heritage Site, combines a series of working environments with international connections, well tended and interpreted horticultural and archival collections and a historic landscape of great importance. Of the other London landscape associated with the 3rd Earl, Caen Wood or Kenwood, we did not consider we had available sufficient material about his influence there to justify a chapter. The gardens of St John's Lodge, approached from the Inner Circle in London's Regent's Park and managed by the Royal Parks, continues to surprise by its intimate, private nature, retaining the feel of how it must have been when used as the private London residence of the 3rd Marquess and his family.

In southern England the gardens of Luton and Highcliffe, related by the plant collections of the 3rd Earl, can be viewed, albeit by different groups of visitors. Luton Hoo House has been converted into a hotel so that its clients have the opportunity of appreciating a landscape moulded by the skills of 'Capability' Brown. The five acre octagonal walled kitchen garden, also designed by Brown, now in different ownership, is undergoing sensitive restoration, much of it carried out by volunteers. The gardens are open to the public on specific occasions throughout the year with a provision of study days and guided tours. The estate of Highcliffe Castle, the successor to the 3rd Earl's precariously poised cliff-top mansion, was rescued by Christchurch Borough Council after a disastrous fire in the house. Its gardens and the land just beyond it are much visited by the public, especially as part of the coastal footpath along this part of Dorset. Within the house can now be viewed, on longterm loan, two paintings by Charles Steuart of the original eighteenth century house.

Robert Peel,
March 2012

For Kitty, Michael, Minnie, James and Nellie

Bute Family

James Stewart
2nd Earl Bute by
William Aikman,
1720.

The Bute family has a distinguished ancestry, being descended from a daughter of King Robert the Bruce in the fourteenth century and from her son, Robert II of Scotland. They played a minor part in the political life of Scottish aristocracy for the next 400 years. It was not until 1703 that Sir James Stewart was made the 1st Earl of Bute and the family moved into another political league. Bute was a member of Queen Anne's Privy Council and, though he had been appointed a commissioner for the union of Scotland with England and Wales, he decided against supporting it and withdrew from Parliament at its inception in 1707. He retired to his family home on the island of Bute and later died at Bath in 1710.

His son James, who altered the family name to Stuart, had a very advantageous marriage in 1711 with Lady Anne Campbell, the only daughter of the 1st Duke of Argyll. The prominence of the Argylls within England and Scotland prompted Bute to build a new house, Mount Stuart, and lay out grounds where his wife could live in the manner to which she was accustomed. Their home in Rothesay, the Old Mansion House, though recently built, was in the High Street and lacked both distinction and a surrounding pleasance. It was not until 1718, however, that James managed to start work on Mount Stuart, after he had received an inheritance from his maternal grandfather. He was even teased by Lady Anne's brother, the Duke, who never believed that the project would get past the planning stage. Work continued over a period of four years.

James was Lord of the Bedchamber to King George I and spent a lot of time away from Bute. Moreover he had little time to enjoy his new house and gardens because he

Previous pages:
John, 6th Marquess,
in front of Mount
Stuart. He initiated
its restoration
programme.

14

succumbed to an illness and died in London in January 1723, aged only 33. His eldest son, John, was a mere nine years old on becoming the 3rd Earl. In a letter to her sister-in-law, the Duchess of Argyll, the widowed countess vowed to live a retired life on Bute, leaving John in London in the charge of a tutor, Mr Gillardy, and keeping her other children with her. James had provided for his widow to be "sole curatrix" to the children with the special advice of her brothers, the Duke of Argyll and Lord Archibald Ilay, along with some other Scottish notables, but it was the Argyll brothers who took care and exerted the most influence on the young earl.

The following year, 1724, John was sent to Eton in the wake of his uncle, Ilay, where he showed great promise of being a scholar after a somewhat slow start, and spent much of his holidays with both uncles. With his zeal for picture-collecting and for architecture which led him to employ many leading architects to build and extend his houses, Argyll was a role model for the young Bute. Ilay undoubtedly nurtured his nephew's passion for natural history, astronomy, mechanics and collecting. In 1723–1724 he acquired land on Hounslow Heath, built there a house, Whitton, and for the next 40 years developed one of the largest and best collections of trees and shrubs in the country. His particularity was exotics from America in which he was helped by Peter Collinson, the merchant and naturalist. He also had a collection of rare birds and beasts as well as an extensive library. John may have spent time there on vacation from Eton, particularly when his mother came to stay.

The uncles were very ambitious for their nephew and Bute was sent to university, first at Groningen and then at Leiden in Holland, where he finally graduated in 1734. He studied law and, it may be assumed, botany, since Leiden had, and still has, a venerable and distinguished botanic garden. Though Carl Linnaeus was not to visit Holland until a few years later, both he and Bute had contacts in common and the same goals in wanting to catalogue and organise the natural world into a 'system'. This was also the year Bute came of age and relieved his mother of the responsibilities of caring for Mount Stuart and for his affairs during his minority.

In 1736 he married Mary Wortley Montagu, an heiress from Yorkshire, against her parents' wishes. Such hostility did not appear to diminish their happy union, which produced six sons and six daughters. Apart from the eldest son, Edward, who died in infancy, all survived their parents. Mary was well regarded for her loyalty in the turbulent years ahead and demonstrated both prudence and tact.

At Mount Stuart, Bute botanised and started his collection of plants while improving his estates and writing a journal of the garden from its beginnings in 1718. Interestingly he had sea-water pumped into the house so that he could indulge in restorative cold baths. Although living on Bute, he was not cut off from the outside world. He corresponded with many scientists including Collinson, who was receiving new plants from Mark Catesby in North America, and kept in touch with Linnaeus through their mutual friend, Isaac Lawson, in Leiden. Bute's reputation as a naturalist must have already been well respected because in 1742, when a small white-flowered tree from Carolina first bloomed in England, it was named Stewartia in his honour. (See frontispiece.) Throughout his life as a scientist he had an obsession with collecting, ordering and classifying the natural world. Alongside his plant acquisitions he collected shells on Bute, and later built up such enormous collections of fossils

and minerals that he employed John Hill to catalogue them. He soon realised that along with accurately naming specimens, a key or way of identifying plants, particularly, needed an ordered system. The development of such a system turned out to be the enduring intellectual rigour of his life.

In 1735 Linnaeus published his *Systema Natura* in Leiden in an attempt to set a standard for cataloguing the natural world. When Linnaeus consulted Collinson about active scientists in Britain before publishing his second volume, Bute's name headed the list as a "master of his method". Bute at first embraced the Linnaean system but, along with others, was critical of its shortcomings without being hostile. He was not very impressed by the state of "natural history science" in England when he finally decided to move to London in 1746 and complained that, though many were planting exotic trees and shrubs, nobody was paying attention to the botany to which he was committed.

In London, the Butes lived in town and at Caenwood, a suburban villa on Hampstead Hill commanding extensive views and owned jointly with the Argylls. They moved in society and soon became part of the coterie around Frederick, Prince of Wales. While Lady Bute became close to Princess Augusta, the friendship between Frederick and Bute was based on their love of architecture, gardens, theatre and picture-collecting. This resulted in Bute's direct involvement with Frederick in the development of his garden at Kew and in him being appointed Lord of the Bedchamber in 1750. When Frederick unexpectedly died the following year, it was to Bute that his widow Augusta turned for friendship and advice. Five years later, Bute was appointed Groom of the Stole which regularised his position as chief advisor to Frederick's son, George, now Prince of Wales. The young George developed a deep emotional and intellectual attachment to Bute, which was cemented when his grandfather, George II, died in 1760. As George III he acceded to the throne and Bute was made a member of the Privy Council.

History has looked more kindly of Lord Bute in recent years. His rapid rise to power and influence over the young King inevitably led to jealousies and politicking behind his back. The lampooning of him by the press because of his opposition to aspects of the war against France and Spain whipped up the fervour of the crowd which jostled and threatened him. His Scottish origins increased the rancour and suspicions of Englishmen at all levels and by name he was associated with the Stuart pretenders to the throne whom the Hanoverians had recently suppressed in the 1745 rising. Rumours abounded about the nature of his relationship with Princess Augusta and, after a brief spell as Prime Minister, he was forced to resign, and retreated in 1763 to his estate at Luton, exhausted and depressed.

During the time he attended the young George at court he felt keenly that he was neglecting his own family of eleven children whom at times he hardly saw at all. He did, however, make sure that they were well-educated, and appointed Adam Ferguson, the philosopher, to tutor them. His wife had inherited part of her father's estates in 1761. She was worth over £1 million with an income of £50,000 per year which was at her husband's disposal. This income equates to between £6 and £8 million at today's values using the retail price index. His new wealth and greater leisure time allowed Bute to commission new houses and gardens and to further his collecting and studying of natural phenomena. His first project was to rebuild his house and develop its grounds at Luton.

3rd Earl of Bute with his secretary Charles Jenkinson by Joshua Reynolds, 1763.

Rioting and rumours hostile to Bute continued in London, making it almost impossible for him to spend time there. Some of his children married well but others became embroiled in scandals which put great pressure on his health. From 1768 he was prompted to make what turned out to be a number of tours of Italy and the continent over the next three years, accompanied by Charles, his fourth and undoubtedly favourite son. His aim was to sightsee with a few learned companions and travel incognito in the hope that he would be left in peace. Serious collecting ensued on this trip. He amassed minerals and fossils, many from Naples where he visited Sir William Hamilton and climbed Mount Vesuvius. There were

John Stuart 3rd Earl
of Bute by Allan
Ramsay, 1760.

architectural drawings and watercolours of the places he visited, paintings, bronzes and
scientific tomes as well as the collection of Italian books of the Sorenzo library. Everything was
crated up and sent back to England to be distributed amongst his houses.

In Scotland Bute was a great patron in many spheres, showing an understanding of
the need to educate and encourage the learning of others in the footsteps of the 3rd Duke of
Argyll. When his uncle died in 1761, Bute and his brother, James Stuart Mackenzie, who was
already deeply involved in Scottish politics, took over Argyll's influence and the patronage of the
universities. Dr John Hope was made professor of botany at Edinburgh and put in charge of its

Mary 3rd Countess
of Bute by Sir Joshua
Reynolds, 1777.

Royal Botanic Gardens, offering Bute a second garden to Kew in which to expand his botanical interests. He helped realise Hope's project to publish a *Flora Scotica* in 1778. He donated books and instruments to Aberdeen University in order to develop it as a centre of practical astronomy and scientific education and, by exchanging fossils with John Walker, Professor of Natural History at Edinburgh, encouraged the first teaching of geology at a British university.

On returning from Italy he bought Highcliffe, an estate overlooking the sea at Christchurch in Dorset, and set about creating a "cottage for the sea air and bathing" in 1775. Effectively he retired there to lead a fairly solitary life and pursue his scientific interests, with his son Charles often his only confidant. It was here he produced the *Botanical Tables*, his great oeuvre, a key designed for ladies to identify British plants. In 1790 he had a fall while plant collecting on the cliffs and damaged his ankle. He never fully recovered and died in London within eighteen months.

By the time of his father's death, Bute's eldest son, Viscount Mountstuart, had already carved out a career as a minor diplomat and politician and was created Baron Cardiff in 1776. Contemporaneously three members of the family had seats in the House of Lords since Lady Bute was a peeress in her own right, Baroness Mount Stuart of Wortley. The 4th Earl succeeded in politics where his father had failed and was elevated to the title of Marquess in 1796. He was brilliant and amusing but also feckless, profligate and irresponsible. Earlier he had made an extensive grand tour of Europe in the 1760s, travelling with James Boswell

John, Viscount
Mountstuart, later
1st Marquess of Bute
by Pompeo Batoni,
c. 1760.

in Italy, before marrying the South Wales heiress, Charlotte Jane, daughter of Viscount Windsor, in 1766.

It was shrewd of him to marry well because his mother's fortune was to be settled on his brother, James, and the Bute fortune was limited. The marriage brought him Cardiff Castle and income from extensive estates in Glamorganshire. He also had political appointments to augment his income, including the role of British Ambassador in Turin and later in Spain. Mountstuart lived a lavish lifestyle and his wife was known to have complained that they lived abroad to save money. After Charlotte's death in 1800 he married Frances, daughter and co-heir of Thomas Coutts, the banker, and enjoyed the expenditure of her money until his death in Geneva in 1814.

His brother, Sir Charles Stuart, was born at Caewood House in 1753 and had a respected military career. He served with distinction on two commissions in America, from where he corresponded with his father, but was deeply critical of the conduct of the war and returned to England in 1779. Despite a fiery temper, an argumentative disposition and pride, which made it difficult for him to accept orders from his superiors, he was re-commissioned as an officer in the wars against Napoleon. A brilliant commander and administrator, he captured Minorca with an inferior number of troops and subsequently became its governor in 1798. On his father's death he inherited Highcliffe but did not have long to enjoy it. He died in 1801, leaving two sons, the elder of whom, Charles, was to have a renowned diplomatic career and rebuilt Highcliffe in an eclectic style.

The 1st Marquess' eldest son, John, born in 1767, showed great promise and became an MP for Glamorgan in 1790. He married Elizabeth Crichton, the heiress and only surviving child of the Earl of Dumfries in 1792. John died in 1794, after a fall from his horse, leaving a baby son, John, and a widow already pregnant with a second son, James. On the death of the 1st Marquess, his grandson the 2nd Marquess had already inherited through his mother the Dumfries titles and estates, including Old Place of Mochrum, adding her name Crichton to Stuart. He had been brought up at Dumfries House but, after his mother's death, was supervised by the 1st Marquess. His education involved extensive

John, 2nd Marquess, on Scalpsie Beach, Isle of Bute, with the mountains of Arran behind. Sir Henry Raeburn, c. 1816.

travelling in Europe where he became friends with the Duke of Orléans, later Louis Philippe, King of the French, and he visited Napoleon at Elba in 1814. Distressingly he was afflicted with an eye disease, which confined him to live quietly at Mount Stuart for the next six years. Though being an imaginative man with a deep sense of responsibility and huge capacity for hard work, the weakness in his sight meant that he shunned fashionable society and appeared dour and remote.

When he was able to manage his myopia, he concentrated his energy on the improvement of his properties and promotion of the welfare of his tenants and dependents, progressing through the year from one estate to the next. He always preferred Mount Stuart to any of his other homes and had a particular interest in agriculture, trebling the arable acreage of his land on Bute. In wanting to see Cardiff rival Liverpool as a great commercial seaport he began to develop Cardiff Docks and from their opening in 1839 until 1922, they were owned and financed solely by the family. Cardiff was the largest of the nineteenth century British towns in whose development a single family played such a crucial role, although the development of the later docks was a drain on their finances.

In 1818 he had married a wealthy heiress, Maria North, daughter of the Earl of Guilford, who brought a great deal of money and some of the North estates to their marriage.

John, 3rd Marquess, with a romanticised backdrop of Cardiff Docks.

Maria was ill through much of her married life and in 1841 died without issue aged 48. Four years later John married Sophia, daughter of the 1st Marquess of Hastings, a one-time Governor-General of India, and six months before Bute's death, at 55, she gave birth to a son, John Patrick. This must have been a terrible blow to his brother, Lord James Stuart, who not only shared a mutual antipathy with his sister-in-law but was deprived at the last moment from inheriting the now vast wealth and lands of the Butes which his brother had developed over the previous 30 years.

On his death in 1848 his son at six months old was considered to be the richest infant in the world and was soon made a ward of Chancery, his mother being appointed guardian.

Lord Ninian
Crichton Stuart,
whose statue stands
in front of City
Hall, Cardiff.

John Patrick was a sickly child, brought up travelling between Mount Stuart, Dumfries House and Cardiff Castle. Until the age of 11 and the death of his mother, he was looked after entirely by women, which is why he was thought shy and diffident. However it is much more likely that the row, litigation and court cases which ensued after his mother's death between his two guardians, Lady Elizabeth Moore and Colonel Charles Stuart, affected him more.

John Patrick schemed with Lady Elizabeth and his trusted retainer, Jack Wilson, to escape to Scotland, where they hid in the Granton Hotel, Edinburgh in the hope of coming under the jurisdiction of Scots law. He had taken against Colonel Stuart who had failed to accompany the body of Lady Bute on the journey to her burial at Mount Stuart with the orphaned Marquess.

The Scots were reluctant to give up one of their richest landowners to the jurisdiction of English law. The question of where he was domiciled was at issue. After a ruling in the House of Lords, Lady Elizabeth conceded her role to Stuart. He wanted John Patrick to have a robust education in England and eventually sent him to Harrow. In the holidays the boy spent time with Lord and Lady Galloway on the Wigtownshire coast in a large and happy family at Galloway House. However John Patrick was astute enough to know that in Scotland he would attain his minority, at the age of 14, and with it certain rights. He successfully petitioned the Courts in Edinburgh who appointed new guardians which diluted Colonel Stuart's responsibilities, particularly for his Scottish estates.

As a child he was precocious with a fascination for ancient history. He had a passion for animals and kept a pet hedgehog and, when at Harrow, a glass hive which enabled him to watch the activity of its bees. At Oxford he studied a wide range of religions and travelled with his tutor to Palestine and the Middle East. This was a preface to his conversion to Roman Catholicism immediately after his coming of age in 1868. His guardians were horrified at the prospect and struggled to prevent it, suggesting that he had come under sinister influences while at university. This was refuted by John Patrick's deep spiritual and intellectual desire to embrace the faith. It caused a sensation and deep disapproval in Scotland and the rest of Britain. Disraeli was supposed to have been inspired by this perceived scandal to write his novel *Lothair*. His conversion to Catholicism became vested after marrying a member of the premier Roman Catholic family in England Gwendolen Fitzalan-Howard, in 1872.

He was a constant traveller, often on board his yachts "Lady Bird", "Kittiwake" and "Christine", encircling Scotland, sailing through the Baltic and around the Mediterranean. He attended the Bayreuth Wagner Festival and the representation of Christ's passion at Oberammergau in Bavaria. His extensive journeys through the Middle East enhanced his fascination with Byzantine art and history. His interests and faith led to an obsession with Palestine and the Holy Land so that, following his funeral, the family immediately embarked for Jerusalem to bury his heart on the Mount of Olives according to his wishes.

His other great obsession was architecture, which encompassed both new buildings and the acquisition of ancient monuments for their preservation. On this he lavished energy, research, and money. He used many architects and artisans to rebuild Mount Stuart after it burnt down in 1877. These included William Burges who redesigned and embellished Cardiff Castle and Castell Coch in the Taff Gorge just north of Cardiff. His need to attend Mass and to guarantee that the service was as he wanted it led him to create chapels at all of his houses. Many were elaborately decorated with Byzantine and religious symbolism.

Essentially John Patrick was a scholar and mystic who enjoyed walking long distances and the solitude which this often brought. In common with the 3rd Earl he sought to study and disseminate his subject, in his case that of liturgical research. His greatest oeuvre was a translation into English of the Roman breviary which was published in 1879. He wrote articles for the *Scottish Review*, which he later bought, gave occasional lectures and supported scholars writing on many subjects.

His early death at 53 in 1900 left a young family of a daughter and three sons. Unlike their father and grandfather, who had both lived fatherless childhoods, they had at least enjoyed a close and loving family life with John Patrick. A great number of building and garden projects were left unfinished when he died including House of Falkland, inherited by his second son, Lord Ninian, who then became the hereditary keeper of Falkland Palace. After a short career as MP for Cardiff he was killed in action in France in 1915, leaving his six-month old son Michael as heir.

John, the 4th Marquess, who was 19 when he inherited, shared his father's compulsion for building. He finished many of his father's projects, most notably at Cardiff Castle and Old Place of Mochrum, as well as initiating many of his own including the Byzantine Chapel of St Andrew in Westminster Cathedral and a substantial restoration of Caerphilly Castle. Though fluent in Welsh, John was primarily a Scot, and so the Bute's association with Wales declined throughout the first half of the twentieth century as their mining and agricultural interests were sold off. A major enthusiasm of his was history. He became president of the Scottish History Society and sought to revive the traditional culture and industries of the Scottish islands. This also led to the founding of the Dovecote studio in Edinburgh in 1912 to produce tapestries along traditional lines, two of which now hang in the marble hall at Mount Stuart.

In 1905 he married Augusta, daughter of Sir Henry Bellingham, who bore him two daughters and five sons. On his death in 1947 he left his estate at Old Place of Mochrum, essentially a farm and shooting estate in the south-west of Scotland, to his third son, David. The eldest son John, the 5th Marquess, immediately gave Cardiff Castle and its grounds to the city. His wife, the former Eileen Forbes, daughter of Lord Granard, had never liked the castle as a residence because of its lack of comfort, and with this gift the Butes withdrew to

John, 5th Marquess, in front of Rock Garden, Mount Stuart, c. 1930.

The 4th Marquess outside Mount Stuart, with grapevines and two children, c. 1908.

Scotland. He had, at an early age, assumed the administration of the estates on Bute, living at Kames Castle before moving, on his accession, into Mount Stuart and making it the family home. His abiding passion was the observation and study of birds and those he had ringed were sometimes found from across the Atlantic. Following its evacuation in 1931 he bought the island of St Kilda as a bird sanctuary, which was given to the National Trust for Scotland after his death in 1956. It is Scotland's first natural World Heritage Site.

His heir, John, the elder of twin brothers, was encumbered with huge death duties, obliging him to sell family property in Cardiff to the City corporation and to eventually transfer three houses designed by Robert Adam on the north side of Charlotte Square, Edinburgh, to the National Trust for Scotland in 1969. These houses were protected when his grandfather, the 4th Marquess, had had the foresight to buy them and preserve the integrity of what could be considered the finest example of eighteenth century classical town planning. The

6th Marquess took after both the 3rd and 4th Marquesses in his love of architecture and its conservation and served as Chairman of the National Trust for Scotland for 25 years. This belied a shy and reserved character, which his duty overcame in serving dynamically both the national and local community. With the support of his second wife, Jennifer, he began to complete many of the projects at Mount Stuart, which had been left unfinished for 80 years.

By the planting of globally endangered forest trees in the arboretum at Mount Stuart for conservation, the idea of planting exotics originally initiated by the 3rd Earl came full circle. The mild and damp climate of Mount Stuart has proved ideal for the family involvement with plants, from the collecting and naming of species in the eighteenth century to the saving of them for the twenty-first. The 6th Marquess died in 1993 just as this project was taking root.

On inheriting the title of 7th Marquess, his elder son, the racing driver Johnny Dumfries, along with his siblings Anthony and Sophie Crichton Stuart, took on the challenge to maintain and exhibit the legacy their family had built up over 300 years. Mount Stuart house was first opened to the public in 1995. An ambitious programme to catalogue and maintain the family archives was begun by building a 'state of the art' computerised filing system. Part of the 3rd Earl's botanical library can be seen in the purple library along with the 3rd Marquess' theological books and others on natural history. The internal house decorations reflect wild nature and the landscape of the island, with botanical and animal adornments and paintings. Family portraits and landscapes within the house are testimony to the family's persistent patronage of the arts. The innovative glass panels leading to the conservatory made by the 6th Marquess and finishes to the Marble Chapel at Mount Stuart are evidence of the later generations' commitment to fulfilling their ancestors' vision for the family home. The stunning new visitor centre emerging from the woods at Mount Stuart shows a keen contemporary support for architecture and its relationship with the landscape.

John, 6th Marquess, c. 1970.

John, 7th Marquess, formerly Johnny Dumfries.

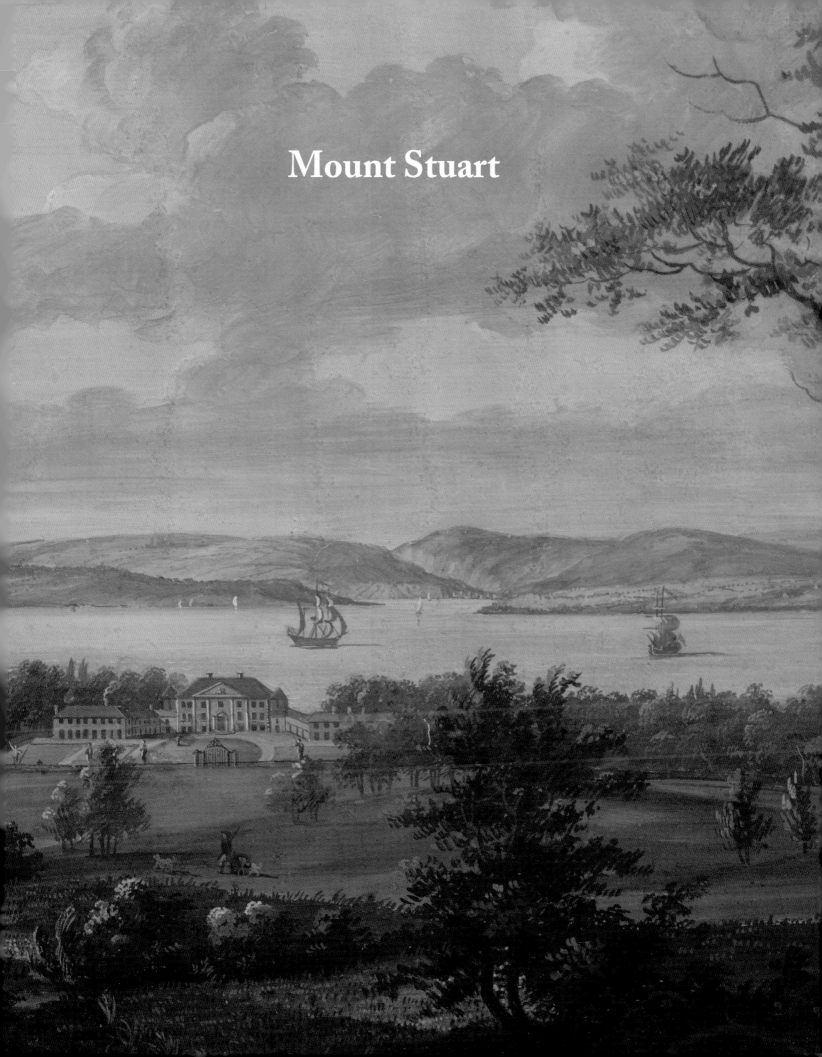

Mount Stuart

Mount Stuart, the principal seat and ancestral home of the Bute family, is on the island off the west coast of Scotland from which they draw their title. The original house five miles south of Rothesay, the island's main town, built between 1718 and 1722 to the designs of Alexander McGill, is surrounded by policies of about 300 acres.* The estate was developed by James, 2nd Earl of Bute, with his wife, Anne, whose brothers, the 2nd and 3rd Dukes of Argyll, were renowned for their building projects and their fine landscaped estates in both England and Scotland. After the sacking of the Butes' previous home, Rothesay castle, in 1685, they moved to a townhouse in Rothesay from where they eventually planned a new house, albeit slowly. This was at a time when many aristocrats, jostling for position at court, were establishing their prestige by creating magnificent houses and gardens.

The original house from the Firth of Clyde. Charles Steuart, 1775.

* In Scotland the term *policies* describes the pleasure-grounds around a mansion.

The position chosen for the house was on a commanding site above a 100 foot cliff looking east across the Firth of Clyde. The quarries which yielded the Old Red sandstone for its construction can be seen on the estate. Timber had to be imported from as far away as Norway, there being no suitable conifers on Bute. Due to the lack of roads on the island at that time, other building materials would have come directly by boat from the mainland. The remains of the original pier at Scoulag lies at the end of the lime tree avenue to the north of the house.

Previous pages: Looking east towards the original house of Mount Stuart backed by the Firth of Clyde. Detail of painting attributed to Charles Steuart, 1781.

With building already in progress, James gave instructions for the grounds to be laid out immediately around the house on the level land above the cliff. The scheme was very much in line with current fashions. In 1718 "Scotch firrs" were planted north and south of the west-facing entrance court, framing the house when viewed from the sea. The principal diagonal paths running from the centre of the east or coastal facade were laid out and planted up the following year, as was the 45 Avenue, the main cross axis in front of the house, named for its width in feet. On that side too a large grassed parterre was enclosed by a lime hedge. The Clyde Walk followed the cliff edge and further walks described a sophisticated geometric pattern. Classic features of this baroque garden included a *patte d'oie*, triple 'cabinets', a wilderness, a labyrinth, a bowling green, a grove and orchards. Trees of beech, lime, elm and plane with hedges of hawthorn and hornbeam were used for the walks and winding paths. Alders and birch occupied the cabinets and were under-planted with flowering shrubs. Below the cliff a beech avenue was flanked with thickets and specimen plane trees on both sides.

Plants came from a variety of sources. William Miller in Edinburgh supplied vegetable and flower seeds as well as 1,000 English elms, 140 *Daphne mezereum*, and 6,000 Dutch alders. Tools and other trees from Mitchell's of Renfrew were delivered from the mainland by the Earl's boatman to the gardener, Alexander McGrigor. To complete the planting of the policies, seven contract gardeners were sent from Edinburgh in 1722 and continued to come for a further six years. Although James died in London the next year, work did not cease. While his widow retired to Bute with their younger children, their eldest son, John, the 3rd Earl, pursued his education in London and Eton.

Miller sent 3,000 hornbeams for the two northern cabinets and 500 horse chestnuts; also holly berries, hornbeam seeds, yew berries, beech mast and a peck of English acorns to be sown in the tree nurseries alongside the kitchen gardens which lay to the north and south of the house. In the kitchen gardens were added a number of fruit trees: "pears, plumbs, apples, fine wall cherries, apricocks, peaches and nectarines". Other deliveries included flowering shrubs and tulip and jonquil bulbs. Conifers were planted extensively from the Racer's Burn in the south to the Harbour Avenue, now the Lime Avenue, in the north. A rowan walk added a particularly Scottish flavour.

By the time the 3rd Earl came of age in 1734 and returned to Mount Stuart the design structure of the grounds was complete. He had been well trained in botany during his four years in Holland, mostly spent at Leiden. His interest in landscaping and gardening was still developing, however, under the influence of his uncle, Lord Ilay, whose plant nursery and garden at Whitton was becoming one of the largest and finest collections of its time. There avenues of Cedar of Lebanon were admired together with the first planting in Britain of several varieties of North American pines and firs. In the stove houses exotics thrived, including the famous paw-paws, *Carica papaya*, which continued to flower every year. A fruitful exchange of ideas and plants developed between uncle and nephew for years.

The 3rd Earl owned Batty Langley's *New Principles of Gardening*, published 1728, and its companion *A Sure Method of Improving Estates*. Langley's advocacy of grading flowering shrubs from the smallest at the front to the largest at the back began to alter attitudes to planting. Such arrangements may seem obvious now but, in the early 1700s, trees tended to be grown in hedged compartments with only their canopies showing. From the 1730s onwards a change in emphasis from foliage to flowers, colours and scents had occurred

with the introduction of new plants from North America. John embraced these ideas in the Mount Stuart gardens and wrote:

> ... I began planting the Ring having grub'd up all the old trees that were not thriving, and put ash Sicamore oak as thick as I could both in the ring thicket and also thatt without the Circular walks. I also cut down the thorn hedge and planted flowring shrubs and trees. In the first row next the ring in the following order, first a horse chestnut then a liburnum then a rown tree; Betwisch each of which I putt a Lilliak which last Does not thrive.

All the trees in the grove were pruned in the spring of 1737 to reduce shading of the flowering shrubs. Clipping of both high and low hedges lasted two months in the summer. For appearance and ease of maintenance, Bute decided that autumn to cut down all the tall hedges except for those in the narrow walks and replace them with hornbeam kept to five feet high. Despite having lightened the tree canopy, the hibiscus still did not flourish and were replanted elsewhere.

The journal that Bute kept of both his and his father's planting schemes document that the position of the house, exposed to winds off the sea on its raised beach of shallow soils, proved a challenge to growing trees. Alders were planted as nurse trees, serving to drain the ground for other species and to enrich the soil by the fixation of nitrogen through their roots. Their purpose completed, they were grubbed up. Unfortunately, the 40,000 five year old conifers planted on the flat ground below the cliff were all killed by drought the following spring. Stones and soil were moved from area to area in the walks to improve drainage and level the surface. On the hill west of the house, later to be called Mount Montague after his wife's family, six tenants were paid "in meal" to prepare the ground for planting and dig a ditch around it. A new stone bridge was made for the carriage drive over Racer's Burn to the south of the house. Gilmoor and his men surrounded the 120 acre deer park to the north with a nine foot wall. Despite Bute's complaints at all the problems, significant work was achieved in that one year of 1737.

Meanwhile, propagation was much practised. 100 shoots of Dutch honeysuckle were layered in the nursery and red daphne berries planted. Seeds of laburnum and bladder senna were collected along with rowan and whitethorn berries to be sown in the tree nurseries. Suckers of lilacs were planted out and a wild cherry placed next to the summer-house. The shell of this house, later in the year to be rebuilt in stone, still remains at the north end of the beech walk below the cliff. Other garden buildings, since lost, include a grotto, a green house, and an eye catcher on Mount Montague. A stable was built near the house. It had accommodation for 15 horses, the first to be introduced to the island.

The ambitions of his uncles for his career inevitably drew Bute back to London where he moved with his family in 1746, eventually to settle at Caenwood, or Kenwood House as it is known today, and never to return to Mount Stuart. McGrigor continued as gardener on a salary of £120 Scots and diligently sent his employer weekly letters. The 1758 report of a survey of the estate drew attention to the urgent need to thin the plantations.

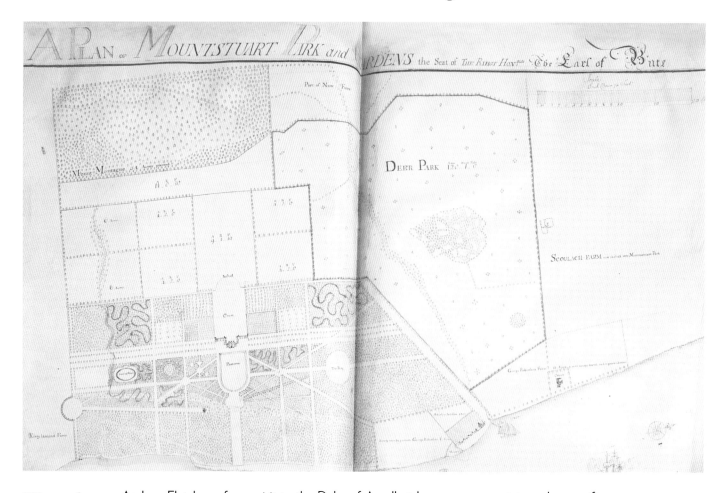

1758 survey of
Mount Stuart by
John Foulis.

Andrew Fletcher, after a visit to the Duke of Argyll at Inverary, was sent to make specific recommendations. These were carried out by the factor, Dunlop, since McGrigor didn't dare—his "heart failed". Every other beech on the lower walk was removed to leave a 30 foot gap. Around the bowling green the elms were thinned to 20 feet apart. Fletcher was delighted at the success of many foreign introductions like the tulip trees, hop hornbeams, acacia and, particularly, a Swedish maple which, at 26 feet high, was taller than the one at Whitton.

Bute continued to send material to Mount Stuart to grow on in his nurseries and grounds. At last almost everything was thriving. The only struggling plantation was on Mount Montague which, according to the surveyor, had a cold weeping spongy moory soil much exposed to the storms. James Stuart Mackenzie, Bute's younger brother, was keeping a watch on the estate and implementing improvements to the house. In 1780 he recommended the surveyor, Peter May, as manager, who kept in constant correspondence with Bute's eldest son, Lord Mountstuart, and reported to him on his occasional visits.

After Bute's death, his son, soon to become the 1st Marquess, began by commissioning a plan for a new kitchen garden some distance north of the house. Though it was not implemented for another 25 years, the old nurseries and kitchen gardens from around the house were gradually removed and the land redesigned. A terrace with a border was laid out in 1799 with a new approach from Lady's Walk. Island beds of shrubs were ordered for the east side of the house, two with a specimen magnolia surrounded by 'foreign' flowers and shrubs and the others with a tulip tree under-planted with low shrubs. Dahlias may well have been amongst those flowers. Charlotte, the Marchioness, had been responsible for introducing such natives of Mexico to Kew in 1798, after procuring seed from Madrid Botanical Gardens. Her husband was Ambassador to Spain at the time.

Two columns at the entrance to the new shrubbery from the north wing were constructed of stones taken from a nearby vitrified fort, laid in an oval shape and layered with shells, pebbles, rock and marine plants. "This if well executed would form a compleat collection of Minerals, fossils, and curious plants of the island and would be seen at one view," wrote the Marquess. A moss house was built on a mount at the end of a vista and surrounded by root chairs placed at random for rustic effect. However, very particular about keeping the grounds looking neat and tidy, the Marquess proscribed the use of 'living' trees as gate posts and insisted that all wood lying about had to be gathered up regularly. The seventeenth century obelisk sundial at the Old Mansion House in Rothesay was moved to a place just south of Mount Stuart house and can now be seen in the centre of the Wee Garden. Greenwich gravel was specified for the walks.

Until the late eighteenth century a ferry boat sailed from Scoulag pier to Largs on the mainland once a week. Visitors to Mount Stuart from Rothesay would also come by boat. Although greater prosperity led to the town being rebuilt, increasing ownership by farmers of a horse and cart and new roads being laid, the shore road was the last to be finished due to difficult negotiations with landowners. In anticipation of its opening the Marquess built a new pier, ferry house, and a half-circle of estate houses with gardens at Kerrycroy, in 1803, as replacements for the old pier and village at Scoulag, further south.

In planting up the shoreline south of Kerrycroy with scattered trees among the rocks and establishing Strawberry trees and laurustinus, *Arbutus unedo* and *Viburnum tinus*, along the cliff edge for romantic effect, he was inspired by a visit to Mount Edgcumbe in Cornwall. In 1807, over 200,000 trees were planted at Mount Stuart, supplemented by acorns sent from his estate at Luton. In 1811 he became very excited at receiving a new variety of larch from Archangel, in Russia, capable of flourishing in thin soil and hopefully on the moor above Mount Stuart. It is probable that today's lime avenue, the former Harbour Avenue, was replanted in 1812, to judge from documentary evidence and the trees' girth. When Thomas White, the English gardener, visited two years later he was astonished to see such a fine place but commented that the old trees might have been larger had they been given sufficient room. This was a recurrent complaint about the management of the trees.

In 1814 the 1st Marquess' grandson, John, Earl of Dumfries, inherited the marquisate as a young man. He devoted himself to improving his estates and promoting the welfare of his tenants. In those first years he spent a great deal of time at Mount Stuart caring for the tree plantations and, after his marriage to Maria North, creating new flower gardens. The new island beds with their shrubs at the front of the house were removed. Towards the new north entrance land was cleared for the new kitchen garden which was walled in 1820 with bricks made on site. Gates and a lodge, designed by William Burn, were built next to Kerrycroy village and adjustments were made to the drive which wound through fields recently brought into the policies, where the Scoulag Burn runs towards the sea.

Limetree avenue.
Early twenty-first
century.

At the end of 1823 land to the south of Racer's Burn was drained and fenced in preparation for a new flower garden, to be known as the "Wee Garden", entered from the 45 Avenue. The Marquess was unwilling to do any planting there until it was secure from the depredations of deer. The plants included a Cedar of Lebanon, a tulip tree, a catalpa, olives, cork oaks and evergreen oaks with flowering shrubs in front. One of the corks still survives today as well as a number of the original winding gravel paths. The central round bed was divided, unusually, into 11 wedges. Weeping willows and roses lined the burn. Over the years a remarkable variety of specimen trees, shrubs and plants have grown in this sheltered garden though now it specialises on those from the southern hemisphere. From the first plantings remain a huge camellia, with a trunk over four feet in girth, reputed to be one of the first grown outside in Britain, and a *Crinodendron hookerianum* from Chile with a height of 30 feet and circumference of 150 feet, one of the finest specimens in Britain.

John Smith, the estate forester and gardener, was planting up woods throughout Bute. Acorns and oak seedlings sent from Luton in their hundreds of thousands would have been those of the English or pedunculate oak *Quercus robur*, less suited to the West of Scotland than its native, the slimmer sessile oak *Q. petraea*. Nevertheless there are a few surviving English oaks within the grounds dating from this time. Smith went on to encourage Scottish landowners to plant up timber with his *Treatise on the Management and Cultivation of Forest Trees* in 1843. This includes long passages about the economics of forestry as well as the best methods of pruning and thinning.

Wee Garden, Mount
Stuart. Early twenty-
first century.

On the 2nd Marquess' death in 1848 his brother became responsible for managing the Scottish estates. On his refusing John's widow, Sophia, and her infant son, John Patrick, the right to use them, she turned for support and advice to Onesiphorous Tyndall Bruce at Falkland, her husband's closest friend, and by 1853 was finally allowed access. She died in 1859 and it was not for another two years, on reaching his minority, that John Patrick was able to exercise some influence over the management of these properties.

The original design structure of the woods on the upper level outside the house no longer existed and a new rectangular bowling green had been laid between the east front and the parterre. Only three avenues remained from the 2nd Earl's scheme: the north diagonal centring on the house, the 45, and the 40 which ended at Racer's Burn in a roundel. John Patrick and his new forester from Edinburgh, John Thomson, opened up green paths and vistas through the woods. The design, in the spirit of the original, resembles a Union Jack. In the middle was erected a column, dedicated to Princess Augusta by the 3rd Earl and brought from Luton in 1872. The Beehive Well, named for its shape, was also created at this time over a natural spring.

In the late 1860s a pinetum was formally laid out in a criss-cross grid on 100 acres to the south of the kitchen garden. Known as the Green Paths, it was planted mainly with exotic evergreens from North America, under which were 3,000 mahonias, 1,000 rhododendrons and holly, yew, privet, laurel and bay. Some of the original Douglas fir, Wellingtonias and pines survive along with naturalised mahonia, but the losses are disappointing and surprising.

Augusta column
in the Woodland
Garden moved from
Luton. Early twenty-
first century.

There are no surviving Cedars of Lebanon, deodars or tulip trees, and only a few monkey-puzzle trees from the original list are known to have survived into the twentieth century. This may have been due to storms, particularly to those in the winter of 1883 when 2,000 trees came down in the policies. Gaps were filled with quick growing Douglas fir, most which have since been felled for timber. The storms also brought down some lime trees in the Lime Avenue which were saved by being topped and pulled back into position. Throughout the island a further 630,000 oak, Scots pine and larch trees were planted at this time as well as a stand of Douglas firs which still grow in the ancient wood of Barmore on the side of Loch Fad.

After his marriage, John Patrick started a menagerie of exotic animals. Porcupines, beavers, wallabies and kangaroos roamed the policies. Rabbits, which he would not allow to be killed, proliferated. Three of the beavers died almost immediately but the fourth escaped to the moor. It was later found to have felled a poplar, made a nest in a pond and eaten the water plants. A second consignment, arriving in 1875, adapted better. Originally housed in a pig-sty they were moved to a large stone-walled pen crossed by a burn, where they succeeded in breeding. However, no amount of care could prevent the dampness of the climate from killing them.

It was his wife who ordered the first kangaroos, even though she was worried they might reach eight feet in height and jump on her. Several species together with wallabies were sent by night mail via Glasgow from Charles Jamrach in London. The price of the large wallaroo, similar to a kangaroo, was £25. Turkeys and many species of exotic pheasants wandered the policies at will. The Lady Amherst pheasants became feral amongst the rhododendrons in conditions similar to their native Burma. Other pheasants had been bred for sport in the grounds from the time of the 1st Marquess. John Patrick eschewed hunting, shooting and fishing. He supported the anti-vivisection movement and banned gin traps on his estates. Late nineteenth century photographs of the garden show flowerbeds netted against rabbit damage although John Patrick was known to have said: "there are really quite a large number of plants that rabbits don't injure".

In 1874 the grounds were opened to visitors provided they left their carriages at the gates and kept to the gravel walks. Names were entered in a book at the North Lodge where a large pair of bronze gates, since removed, lent majesty to the entrance. The visitor marvelled at the lush sheltered woodland while progressing under the overhanging trees of the lime avenue and passing tall bamboos and many coloured rhododendrons. The total length of the walks was almost nine miles.

A catastrophe occurred in December 1877. The house caught fire and was so badly damaged that John Patrick decided to commission a new building from the distinguished Edinburgh architect Robert Rowand Anderson. Fortunately most of the contents were rescued and the newly designed chapel by William Burges unaffected. A railway specially laid from Kerrycroy harbour to transport materials and decoration up to the house, many crafted in the Cardiff workshops, was not finally removed until 1886. The house is portentously Gothic, influenced by modern ideas of historicism from the Continent, but its strident pink bulk sits uneasily in the landscape, out of balance with the surrounding woods. Perhaps in an effort to let it adapt more comfortably to its setting a number of new garden projects were commissioned in the grounds at the end of the initial building works.

The disruption caused by the building required the complete relaying of the large parterre. Vines and wisteria covered the east side of the house in front of which a number of flowerbeds alternated with statues. West of Mount Montague on land which adjoined a new road from Kerrycroy to Kingarth, Mr Heron, the head gardener, used the course of the Scoulag Burn to create a series of ponds and gardens in 1893. Though now completely overgrown, limes, elms and beech still define the structural planting under which appear rhododendrons, yellow iris and Japanese knotweed. John Patrick would wind his way up through the woods on Mount Montague to pass through this garden as he walked the moor road into Rothesay. The last pond, known as the Moss, was where he played curling with his neighbours. On one occasion, at dusk, footmen brought out candles to illuminate the end of the game. When temperatures dropped to freezing, a series of sluices controlled the flooding of the pond so that its surface could systematically glaze over and then allow for the thawed waters to escape. This pond is now invaded with alders. Failing confidence in Mr Heron's landscaping skills persuaded the Butes to look elsewhere for the designer of a rock garden and path with religious symbolism to be called the Calvary Walk. In 1895 they chose Thomas Mawson.

Mawson had set up Lakeland Nurseries beside Windermere in the 1880s with his brothers. This business became extremely successful at creating heath, rock and woodland gardens incorporating streams and pools. Before his involvement at Mount Stuart, rocks had been placed on the plain grass slope behind the house as a focus of interest. An artificial

rivulet, fed by a pipe from the Scoulag Burn about half a mile away, dropped in a series of cascades and was crossed by several miniature bridges. In the autumn of 1895, Mawson was taken by John Patrick's daughter to look at this site and that of Racer's Burn where her father wanted to develop his Calvary Walk. Mawson later wrote that the rock garden ought to have an airy spaciousness about it, with massing of plants to imitate nature, which 'does not dot about'. Pursuing this idea he planted heaths, low shrubs and grasses further up the slope while below it a waterfall dropped over the lip of a dam of large, cemented stones into a lily pond. This dramatic landscape, reinforced with the sound of trickling water, still greets visitors as they arrive at the *porte cochère* of the house.

The Calvary Walk was one of his finest landscape creations but unfortunately no plans survive. Mawson described the location as "a swamp, trodden into disagreeable mud by cattle". By varying the flow of the burn into pools, cascades and small waterfalls with the use of boulders from surrounding woods, Mawson sculpted the land with the help of his foreman, Calder. He described it as: "... most beautiful, and much more like generous, wayward nature than the stream as we found it". Under the existing beeches and birches meandering woodland walks were laid out using native shrubs and bushes as well as iris and cardiocrinums from the Himalayas. Great care was taken to move the rocks into position with their mossy cover intact. Ferns and perennials from the wild were planted in their gaps and fissures.

John Patrick was delighted, all the more so since the religious significance of the project was to be emphasised in plans drawn up by Mawson's partner, Dan Gibson. An oratory at each of the 12 stations-of-the-cross would serve to commemorate Christ's ordeal in bearing his own cross to the site of his crucifixion on Calvary Hill. A Church of the Holy Sepulchre, inspired by that in Jerusalem, and a thirty-foot high crucifix silhouetted against the sky were also planned. By the time John Patrick died in 1900 only the paths were in place. Apart from a life-size statue of Jesus, in tin, placed in the centre of the Wee Garden and now at the chapel by the shore, nothing remains of this vigorous assertion of his Christian faith.

Calvary Walk, c. 1900 Thomas Mawson's masterpiece.

Robert Weir Schultz worked at Mount Stuart too, designing some of its furniture made at the Cardiff workshops and supervising the installation of its electrical fittings: the house was the first in Scotland to be lit by electricity. He was the architect of Scoulag Lodge at the entrance to a drive connecting with the new road to Kingarth. Although inspired by a Scottish tower house in an Arts and Crafts tradition its architectural elements are too ambitious for its size. He also created the steps to the bowling green and designed a mortuary chamber in the church at Scoulag where John Patrick was buried in a velvet-covered coffin within a white marble sarcophagus.

A solemn blessing of a 10 foot high marble crucifix took place when John, the 4th Marquess, on achieving his majority in 1902, carried out the wishes of his father that one should be erected where he died and another where he was interred. The crucifix at Mount Stuart was erected on a boulder overlooking the site where Racer's Burn disgorges from the cliff face and was secured with steel hawsers. After being damaged it was taken down and buried somewhere in the policies awaiting repair, but no exact record was kept of its location.

Unlike their father, John and his brothers were keen on shooting game and already by 1899 pheasants were being reared for shoots at the north end of Bute and on the island of Cumbrae. It was not long before somewhere on the estate a small party would go out shooting on most days from November to late January. Roe deer, grouse, pheasants and surprisingly 15 swans are recorded in the game book! The refrain was said to be: "My friends, it is a fine day: let us go out and kill something." The most successful year was 1913 when 4,860 red grouse, 418 woodcock and 303 snipe were bagged. A pretty, circular game larder was built to the south of the house when the existing meat safe became too small. Rabbits, a continuous pest, were controlled by ferreting and shooting and also provided meat for the farmers. Enterprises

CHAPEL MOUNT STUART, ROTHESAY.

Early twentieth century postcard view of the Chapel at Scoulag.

of a more commercial nature included a trout hatchery, set up in Loch Fad with the intention of letting the fishing, and a lobster hatchery, beginning to be productive by 1914.

During the First World War the house became a naval hospital. A significant threat to its survival came in 1920 when John put it up for sale on condition it be removed for re-erection elsewhere as a hydro or casino. He had become increasingly depressed about the effects of political change throughout the world, the estate's annual surfeit of expenditure over income of £5,000, growing taxation liabilities and the provision of adequate funds for his heirs to settle his own death duties. Since no buyer could be found, the house was closed up and a visitor was saddened by Mount Stuart's semi-dismantled and neglected state. Happily a programme of planting exotics was continued throughout the twentieth century in the Wee garden.

In 1947, the 4th Marquess died. The 5th Marquess was living in nearby Kames Castle with his wife and family. They decided to re-open and move back to Mount Stuart. The overgrown rock garden was cleared and initially planted up with red and yellow begonias and tulips. Under Jock McVey, the head gardener, there was an arrangement to receive unusual specimens from the Royal Botanic gardens in Edinburgh to be planted in the Wee Garden. The Japanese umbrella pine, *Sciadopitys verticillata*, now 60 feet high and eight feet in girth, along with the rare *Magnolia campbellii*, whose low hanging branches allows visitors to smell its flowers in March, were both planted by him.

Throughout the policies, cutting back the wild rhododendrons, clearing the weed-trees and attending to the drainage became an annual winter routine for the estate under John, the 6th Marquess. Despite his care for the trees of Mount Stuart, the beech avenue, though felled in the 1960s, was not to be replanted until 1995. This was done with the help of local school children and focussed attention on the partially restored summer-house at its northern end. In clearing the Racer's Burn of vegetation and dredging the ponds, the Calvary Walk was revealed and its forgotten paths resurfaced. A new pond was created below the cliff

Kitchen Garden and Pavilion, 2000.

near where the burn flows out to the sea. An avenue of *Cryptomeria japonica*, grown from seed reputed to have come from the Forbidden City in Beijing, was planted at the south end of the 45 Avenue to replace its red horse chestnuts.

In 1988, John and his second wife, Jennifer, bought an octagonal glass pavilion from the Glasgow garden festival as the centrepiece for a new initiative in the walled garden. Rosemary Verey, the garden designer, with Paul Martin, the head gardener, planned a decorative and productive *potager* around it for the education and delight of visitors. The two wide gateways which pierced the remaining high brick wall on the north side were redesigned by the Edinburgh architect, Stewart Tod, who also added decorative finials to the pavilion. There were separate ornamental areas for culinary and medicinal herbs, cut flowers for the house, fruit cages, vegetables and an orchard. Tender plants give an elaborate allure to the pavilion and elsewhere.

The Butes, both deeply interested in plants, embraced the idea of collecting and displaying exotic species within the grounds once again. The Rock Garden became a focus for Asiatic plants, many of which Jennifer brought back from plant hunting expeditions,

Fitzroya cupressoides.

including *Michaelia dolopsa and wilsonii*. The sheltered Wee Garden with the magnificent Chilean *Crinodendron hookerianum* as a centre piece is now being planted with southern hemisphere species, including endangered monkey puzzle trees, *Araucaria araucana*, though retaining those established specimens too mature to transplant. Graham Alcorn, the botanist gardener, is particularly excited that the *Banksia integrifolia*, planted in 1995 from Jennifer's collection, set seed for the first time in 2006.

Incorporating the Green Paths pinetum 150 acres of woodland were set aside, in 1990, as the flagship site for a conifer conservation programme run by Martin Gardner at the Royal Botanic Gardens in Edinburgh (RBGE). Collections of young trees, threatened with extinction in their native habitats, were planted in geographic zones. This living seed bank will preserve the gene pool of these particular conifers, which include several distinct specimens of *Fitzroya cupressoides*, close to extinction in their native Patagonia due to excessive felling. This species was originally collected by William Lobb in 1869 and brought to Britain. Of the fine original trees which he grew, almost all are the same clone, making them more vulnerable to survival and stressing the need to plant genetically diverse stock for long-term conservation.

In 1989 the Mount Stuart Trust was incorporated to preserve the house and grounds as an integral unit and maintain the rural lifestyle of the entire 28,000 acre estate, about 90 per cent of the island. Its aim is to provide public access to Mount Stuart and promote education of its architecture, art and botany. Though a new type of enterprise for the family it is consistent with their historical approach to the extensive commissioning and collecting of new works. The house was opened in 1995 after an extensive conservation and restoration programme, initiated by the 6th Marquess and continued by his children John, the 7th Marquess, and siblings Anthony and Sophie Crichton Stuart.

In 2001 a new visitors' centre designed by Alfred Munckenbeck was opened. Uninterrupted hardwood louvers clothe the walls above which an upper floor with its seemingly frameless glazing accommodates a restaurant conceived for visitors to have the sense of being suspended in a tree house on the edge of a wood. Its flat roof appears to hover above with no apparent supports. Its north garden, through which visitors progress from the car park, was designed by James Alexander Sinclair, with strong verticality to contrast with the horizontal

The award-winning visitors centre with Paperclip Garden in 2008.

lines of the building. According to Sinclair it is based on the idea of an unfurled paperclip with wide parallel lines of planting including *Thalictrum rochenbruneanum*, and the grasses *Miscanthus 'Ferne Osten'* and *Carex buchananii*. To overcome damage by rabbits the design is in the process of being modified. The garden on the south side is planted to blend in with the wood. Sinclair has also rationalised plantings within the kitchen garden. As the family have not been in permanent residence at Mount Stuart since the death of the 6th Marquess in 1993, the function of the potager to provide produce for the house has become redundant. By planting up more *Crocosmias* and large stands of *Stipa arundinacea* and *Knautia macedonia* Sinclair has added to the colour and drama of the garden.

Sophie Crichton Stuart has been curating a contemporary visual arts programme at Mount Stuart since 2001 to bring art of an international standard to the island. The house and its history, the landscape and its botanical variety are used as the basis for new works commissioned annually from emerging or mid-career artists. Many are temporary exhibits within the gardens. The programme began with a land drawing from Kate Whiteford called *Shadow of a Necklace*. This dramatic white unclasped necklace, cut into the parterre lawn at Mount Stuart, was only properly appreciated from the second floor of the house, and had associations with eighteenth century historic garden ideals. Anya Gallaccio's Silver Seed exhibition, included the covering of an Austrian pine in the pinetum with silver leaf. Entitled *Begin again to the summoning birds*, it was on show in 2005. The next year Nathan Coley's

Land Art project, *Shadow of a Necklace*, 2001, by Kate Whiteford, seen from an upper window in the house.

lettering on scaffolding across the 40 Avenue and in view of the Burges chapel was illuminated in light bulbs. It alluded to complex connections between the family, religion and church symbolism and was subsequently shortlisted for the 2007 Turner Prize. This art in the landscape, despite its temporary nature, has sparked much debate. In 2007 Sarah Staton's *In situ ex situ*, botanical drawings, a large scale map representation and wood sculptures, were a response to Martin Gardner's conifer conservation project at Mount Stuart for RBGE, and the Family's commitment to exotic arboriculture throughout the centuries.

The 7th Marquess' stewardship is more keenly commercial, investing in the infrastructure of both rural as well as agricultural and residential properties. His strong emotional attachment to where he was born and raised and his responsibility as head of a family associated with this clearly defined island community for 800 years defines his style of management. His passion for the house, its architecture and historical associations underpins the commissioning of new works in the visitors centre and visual arts programme. Public interaction with the installations forms part of this philosophy, especially Lee Mingwei's *Trilogy of Sounds*, 2010, a large bronze and wood wind chime sculpture, suspended from a tree, which could be viewed from below and within, bombarding the senses with the changing echoes of nature. The last 300 years have seen fluctuations in the degree of commitment to the estate but opening the house and policies to the public has concentrated more attention than ever before on its continued preservation and the community it supports.

Lee Mingwei, *Trilogy of Sounds*, 2010.

Kew

There is no doubt that the Royal Botanic Gardens of Kew would not have existed without the driving enthusiasm and collecting habits of John, the 3rd Earl of Bute, their first director. This spurred Princess Augusta, mother of George III, to continue developing the gardens, begun by her late husband, Prince Frederick, from 1751 until her death in 1772. However, the gardens of 330 acres we know today are very much larger than those of the Princess. They are an amalgamation in 1802 of two Royal estates, Kew to the east and Richmond Lodge on the west bordering the River Thames. In the eighteenth century they were divided by Lovers Lane, a public road following roughly the course of today's Holly Walk. Its name has a delicious irony since the respective royal owners each side entertained a mutual dislike for each other.

The estate and lodge at Richmond had been bought in 1719 by the Prince of Wales, the future George II, after being banned from the royal residences by his father, George I. Its gardens were adorned with orange trees in tubs and a summerhouse with 18 gilded urns. Caroline, his wife, brought up at Charlottenburg in Germany, was a cultivator of gardens and men: Alexander Pope, the poet living nearby at Twickenham, and garden designers Charles Bridgeman and William Kent. They developed there one of the first 'English landscape' gardens where Kent's Tuscan temple was built on a mound created when Bridgeman cut a

Lake and garden in 1759 by Johan Jacob Schlach.

Previous pages: Swan boat made for Prince George's seventeenth birthday in 1755, which could hold ten people.

50

canal close to the riverside. A grass terrace bordered with elms stretched north to Kew village and became a fashionable promenade on Sundays. In the garden was a classical dairy house with a rectangular pond at the head of the canal, Merlin's thatched cave, the Hermitage displaying six busts of Worthies and a menagerie of tigers and civet cats, all for the delight of Caroline. Bridgeman also typically created a wilderness and an amphitheatre.

When the Prince of Wales acceded to the throne as George II in 1727 his eight children were reunited, the four eldest having been brought up separately by George I. The need for additional accommodation resulted. The Queen rented houses at Kew, including the Dutch House, now Kew Palace, remodelled for her daughters, their extended family and staff. Prince Frederick, now Prince of Wales, had been brought up in Hanover away from his parents and siblings since 1714, arriving in England in December 1728, aged 21. Wanting his own summer residence he purchased a lease on the estate of Kew House, opposite the Dutch House, from Lady Elizabeth Capel in 1731. He had commissioned Kent to begin work there the previous year who added a magnificent new south facade. Rendered and whitewashed, it gave a dazzling new look to this red brick house, subsequently re-named the White House. Inside, Kent designed fabulous decorations and furniture. Lady Elizabeth's German gardener,

White House looking out towards the lake at Kew. Johan Jacob Schlach, 1959.

John Dillman, was kept on to manage the ten-acre gardens, embellished with "pedestalls & marble statues at the East End of Grass Walk" in 1734 but not otherwise redesigned. 24 statues in the garden were given three coats of paint, and trees from Virginia planted.

At first relations between the royal households were cordial, but George II's parsimony and jealousy soon drove a wedge between them. Frederick had been permitted to marry Augusta of Saxe-Gotha in 1736 and the birth of their first child, Augusta, in 1737 at St James's Palace, and not at Hampton Court as the King had commanded, proved to be the catalyst for their estrangement. The Wales's were banished from the royal palaces. Even when dying later that year, the Queen refused to see her son again despite their summer residences being adjacent to each other across Lovers Lane. Frederick and Augusta retired to Kew to lead a country life and bring up their children. Lack of sufficient funds for further improvements at Kew, apart from work on the icehouse, did not preclude their leasing Cliveden. Both these properties

Plan of the Royal Manor of Richmond by Thomas Richardson, 1771.

had farms attached to them where fruit and vegetables were grown for the table, Frederick having a particular appetite for cherries. The painter, Joseph Goupy, not only designed garden seats and other rustic furniture together with buildings for the gardens but gave art lessons to Augusta and the children. In 1748 Frederick decided to transform the gardens at Kew under the influence of the Earl of Bute whom he had met at Egham races the year before.

The earl had divided his life between Mount Stuart and London following his marriage in 1736 and election as a Scottish peer in Parliament. Some of this time was occupied exchanging plants and theories with his uncle Lord Ilay, later 3rd Duke of Argyll, living at Whitton on the river Thames in Teddington, and a circle of plant collectors including Argyll's friend, the merchant and naturalist Peter Collinson. By 1742 Bute was sufficiently admired for his knowledge of plants that the botanists Mark Catesby and Dr Isaac Lawson in Leiden wrote to Linnaeus suggesting that a newly arrived shrub from America, which had recently flowered in Catesby's London garden, be named after him: *Stewartia malacodendron* (see frontispiece). Bute's family name was given its old way of spelling by Linnaeus but, according to botanical rules, could not be subsequently altered. Despite attempts in the nineteenth century to change it to 'Stuartia', the genus is still written as *Stewartia*.

With the loss of his Scottish parliamentary seat at Westminster Bute left for Scotland for five years to concentrate on his scientific studies and develop the gardens and plant collections at Mount Stuart. Though he kept up a lively correspondence with his botanical friends, the island's isolation led to depression. In 1746 the Butes decided to return to London, moving into Kenwood near Hampstead, or Caenwood as it was known then. Lady Bute's mother wrote "I very well remember Caenwood House, and cannot wish you in a more agreeable place. It would be a great pleasure to me to see my grandchildren run about in the gardens. I do not question Lord Bute's good taste in the improvements round it or yours in the choice of furniture."

Bute is thought to have built the Orangery and collected many specimens for the gardens which extended to eight acres, describing them as "every exotick our climate will protect, & considering I have not had but one year, the number is very great". He was already known to have sponsored plant-hunting expeditions and would regularly receive boxes of new plants from distant lands to catalogue, study, propogate and grow on. It is also clear from correspondence, particularly with Collinson living nearby at Mill Hill, that he had a reputation for plant classification. Specimens would be sent to him for identification. His letters are full of descriptions of the different parts of flowers and plants and their comparison with others previously described. From Caenwood he wrote to Collinson:

> I send you these of the Cytisuses and Coluteas that are in my garden. Some of them I do not find Linnaeus, Haller or Royen have described. *Cytisus Neapolitanus—petioles foliis brevioribus, calycibus squamula duplici auctis, ramulis striates erectis.* This is the plant I got for the ever-green or Neapolitan Cytisus. I cannot find it described in any author; at least so as to make me certain of it. You know it well, so I need not tell you it grows from five to seven feet high. Towards the top of the stalks and leaves are covered with whitish hair. So are the pods. *The pedunculi are foliosi....*

A view of the lake,
island, temples and
Orangery in 1763.

It seems inevitable that when they met in 1747 and became friends, the Prince would share some of the earl's enthusiasm for plant collecting and gardening, and the following year was when Frederick started planning for Kew. At this time the gardens were limited to the area immediately around the White House but Frederick had a farm of about 50 acres and subsequently leased another 40 for his new project. His intentions beyond planting exotic trees from America and the Far East were to make an ornamental aqueduct and then a Mount Parnassus from the excavated spoil upon which would be a temple designed by Joseph Goupy adorned with the busts of philosophers after the manner of its prototype at Stowe. 13 statues by the Florentine sculptor Pietro Francavilla were ordered from the Villa Bracci in Italy but, not arriving until after Frederick's death, were never used in this scheme.

Plans for the garden, drawn by Giovanni Niccolò Servandoni, a designer of garden features such as at West Wycombe, were approved by both the Prince and Princess but do not survive. The landscaping at Kew was made into a social event with planting shared with courtiers, women and even children. While supervising some work in March 1751, Frederick was drenched by a sudden hailstorm. The subsequent chill and treatment he received from his doctors proved fatal and within three weeks he was dead. Writing about this tragedy, Collinson suggested that, despite a long-term interest in gardening and planting, the Prince had recently been spurred on to "excel all others". Dr John Mitchell, a colleague of Bute, wrote that "planting and botany would be the poorer for his passing." Losing both income and position at court was a setback for Bute, though his friendship with Frederick had been time-consuming, particularly after he was made Lord of the Bedchamber in 1750. It had left him little time to carry on with his "favorite studdys", the collecting, identifying and recording of plants. Bute again had the opportunity to return to his science which he felt was much neglected by both gentlemen and intellectuals in Britain.

In 1754 Bute sold Caenwood and leased a house, now called Cambridge Cottage, on Kew Green. His absorption with the gardens at Kew on the other side of his new home's garden wall and the need for financial restraint were factors in the move. It is possible that he already had in mind to develop Kew into a botanic garden. Ever since his student days at Leiden he may have nurtured the ambition to create his own botanic collection, and this was the first realistic opportunity to present itself, combining the necessary ingredients for success: sheltered site, proximity of like-minded collectors, ready availability of incoming exotic plant material from abroad and potential for royal patronage.

With the young Prince of Wales, the future George III, now living at Kew Palace, Bute was well placed to offer his advice to both son and mother. Princess Augusta, also a good friend of Lady Bute, had come to rely on Bute's counsel and judgement in pursuing her husband's plans for the garden and indeed Bute may have brought his collection of plants from Caenwood to Kew. In surrounding herself with advisors like Dr Stephen Hales, curate of Teddington, who was appointed her chaplain in 1751, Augusta showed how serious was her intent in the project. Hales had been a friend of her husband, was a Fellow of the Royal Society, author of *Vegetable Staticks*, a botanical work, and he moved in the same scientific circle as Bute and Argyll at nearby Whitton.

John Dillman remained looking after the kitchen garden where an additional greenhouse was built, while Robert Greening, son of the gardener at Richmond, was taken on

to manage the expanding pleasure grounds and the Princess's herd of cows. He straightway dredged the six acres lake, then levelled and landscaped the grounds between it and the White House from which to improve the views back to the lake from the house. He erected a Chinese temple and a small bell temple in the flower garden in 1754. A few years later a Gothic cathedral in canvas and wood, designed by John Muntz, was placed in a grove. For use on the lake, George was presented on his seventeenth birthday in 1755 with a pleasure barge in the shape of a swan with its "feet so artfully contrived as to supply the place of oars". By now the entire 110 acres had been enclosed with walls and fences and so a flock of sheep could be used to crop and fertilise the lawns. Bute was praised for diversifying a flat, inward looking site with small hillocks and discrete points of interest. Clearly in charge of operations, it was he who, on Robert Greening's death in 1758, appointed John Haverfield from Twickenham as the gardener with a new house on Kew Green. Haverfield and his son were later to take over the additional management of Richmond gardens. A year on and Bute also employed William Aiton, a Scot trained under Philip Miller at the Chelsea Physic garden, specifically to look after the botanic garden on its initial four acres site. This separation of botanical responsibilities from those for the pleasure grounds emphasised the importance that Bute placed on plant collections and was adopted by him at Luton some years later.

   William Chambers produced plans to build a large heated house for tender plants from warmer climates sent or brought by Bute's contacts in Asia, Africa, America and the Continent. Known as the Great Stove, 114 feet long and divided into three sections, its flues

The Orangery, completed in 1761.

were designed by the Rev. Hales. Chambers had been employed in 1757 by Bute, initially to tutor the then Prince of Wales in architecture and drawing and only later to design garden buildings at Kew. He had travelled widely, particularly in China where he had been inspired to write his book *Designs for Chinese Buildings*. Augusta had admired his designs for a mausoleum to Frederick drawn a few years earlier, though the building was never executed.

Temple of the Sun in the arboretum by GE Papendick, c. 1820.

In 1763, after overseeing the construction of the 18 buildings he designed, he published their plans with a map illustrating their disposition in the grounds and sent Bute, despite his fall from political grace, the original drawings at Christmas of that year writing: "I beg pardon for taking this liberty and am with the warmest sentiments of Gratitude for the many Great and generous favours you have conferred upon me."

Chambers was indebted to Bute for the introduction to Princess Augusta and the present king which had underpinned his career. He paid further tribute to Bute in the text accompanying the plans:

> The Gardens are not very large. Nor is their situation by any means advantageous: as it is low, and commands no prospects. Originally the ground was one continued dead flat: the soil was in general barren, and without either wood or water. With so many disadvantages it was not easy to produce anything even tolerable in gardening: but princely munificence, guided by a director equally skilled in cultivating the earth, and in the politer arts, overcame all difficulties. What was once a Desert is now an Eden.

The Aviary Garden in 1772, from the *Universal* magazine.

On his map, close to the White House and facing south was the Orangery, finished in 1761 and sheltering citrus trees for the proceeding 80 years. From there through the arboretum was reached the Temple of the Sun, with fluted columns resting on a stepped plinth, surviving until crushed by a lightening-struck cedar in 1916. Nearby was the Great Stove overlooking the botanic garden, lasting until 1861 and latterly housing the New Zealand collection. It is now marked by an iron frame with a wisteria from the early nineteenth century draped over its eastern side. On passing under an arch was an aviary and the 20 outer and four inner beds of the flower garden surrounding a baroque goldfish pool, all encircled by mature trees. Beside this garden was the menagerie, where an octagonal chinoiserie pavilion occupied the centre of an oval pool with pens around the perimeter. Already by the 1780s this was converted into a lawn.

Above the menagerie on a mound created by excavating the lake and looking south towards it rose the Temple of Bellona, its Doric order decorated with military allusions. Moved in 1803, it now stands inside the Victoria gate. The Temple of Pan, an eye-catcher at the end of a tree-lined path, was allowed to fall into ruins and demolished in 1844. On another higher mound and in a more open position stood the Temple of Aeolus, completely rebuilt, except without its revolving seat, by Decimus Burton in stone in 1845 and still there. Close by was the House of Confucius, originally designed by Goupy in 1749 but repaired by Chambers. It was re-sited at the eastern end of the lake and demolished in 1844. Of the remaining buildings Chambers had erected further south in the pleasure grounds, including the Temple of Victory commemorating the Battle of Minden and now replaced by the flagstaff, just the ruined arch and the iconic Pagoda survive. The arch was deliberately

Ruined arch, 1763.

designed as a ruin; above it was a walkway for driving sheep and cattle from the Kew Road into fields south of the lake. These were separated from the pleasure walks by a ha-ha. In a grouping beside Munz's Gothic cathedral were placed the Alhambra and the Mosque, all of which have since disappeared.

The Pagoda, with its green and white striped roofs fashioned from iron, its tinkling bells and 80 dragons on the roof hips, caused a public sensation since it could be seen from outside the garden. It was supposed to have been modelled on a pagoda in Nanjing, China, of which Chambers may only have seen an image. Excepting the Pagoda, and the Orangery and Great Stove, which were functional, most of Chambers's buildings were built in wood, cleverly disguised to appear more solid. Cheaper to construct, they inevitably required more maintenance. Queen Charlotte, George's teenage consort, was so delighted by the follies that she asked Bute to send a copy of the plans to her family in Mecklenburg and examples of them began to appear in German gardens.

Though Kew was very much his mother's garden, the Prince would have been party to its expansion since he lived next door at Kew Palace and Bute was now advisor to them both. A subtle change occurred in 1760 when his grandfather died and George III came to the throne, aged 22. The new king's reliance on Bute, who was already negotiating the buying of his pictures and medal collection throughout Europe, became even more dependent and Bute was appointed a Privy Councillor. Moreover, as Queen mother, Augusta would not only have increased resources to spend on the gardens but earned the additional cachet to attract even more unusual and rare botanical specimens for Kew. The careful organisation and planning of the gardens, which Bute had put in place when he first took over as director, would now reap its rewards and even more plants came from around the world. When Argyll died in 1761 some of the rarest trees and other plants from his nine acres of garden at Whitton were transplanted at Kew the following spring. Added to the arboretum around the Temple of the Sun, thereby honouring Argyll, was a Cedar of Lebanon, a cork oak and a Kentucky

Previous pages: Temple of Victory by GE Papendick, c. 1820.

62

coffee tree *Gymnocladus dioca*, introduced to Whitton in 1748. Also known to survive from their move from Whitton are the false acacia *Robinia pseudoacacia* and oriental plane *Platanus orientalis* planted for protection beside the wall of the White House and now standing alone. The arboretum, circled by a gravel walk, was where the first known *Aucuba japonica* was grown in Britain, along with the oldest surviving *Ginkgo biloba*, planted up against the Great Stove for protection, and a sophora *Styphnolobium japonicum*, the only one left of five sent by James Gordon from China. The giant *Magnolia acuminata* on the Orangery lawn and the magnificent purple beech on the Broad Walk may also be from this period. Both are species Bute planted in his collection at Highcliffe.

Dr John Hope, Professor of Botany at Edinburgh, had corresponded with Bute and came south for a visit in the late summer of 1766 to learn about new plants and obtain seeds and cuttings to take back to Scotland. Among his contacts were Aiton at Kew and James Lee of Vineyard Nurseries, Hammersmith, previously the gardener at Whitton. In the greenhouses at Kew, which he commented were covered with overlapping oilcloths, were proteas from South Africa and a banana tree in fruit. He noted that oleanders were propagated by layering inside the greenhouses and admired fine specimens of *Gardenia flore pleno*, which he considered the "most difficult plant yet introduced". Outside he remarked that the bog area was lined with clay and trees, planted in the pleasure grounds, were protected from sheep with stakes arranged in an inverted cone. On a one acre site, a quarter of the four acres physic garden herbaceous plants were arranged according to the Linnaean system in long order beds with a path between every pair, each plant label showing the genus by name and the species by number.

The Pagoda, completed in 1762.

Gingko biloba, transferred from Whitton in 1762. With its hardiness unknown, it was originally planted against the wall of the Great Stove, whose demolition in 1861 left the tree free-standing.

Pagoda Tree
(*Styphonolobium
japonicum*),
previously *Sophora*,
one of Kew's "Old
Lions", transplanted
from Whitton
in 1762, only a
few years after its
introduction into
the country. It is
now supported by
metal struts.

Bute was keen to record all the plants in the collection and the first *Hortus Kewensis*, a catalogue naming 3,400 species growing at Kew, was published in 1768 by protege and fellow scientist John Hill. He had written a number of botanical works of which *Eden: A Complete Body of Gardening* was dedicated to Bute when published in 1757. The next year he suggested in a pamphlet that there should be a botanical garden at Kensington Palace where sometime later, due no doubt to Bute's patronage, he was appointed its gardener at £2,000 per annum. Hill also retained some unofficial role at Kew. About the same time they began to collaborate on producing *The Vegetable System*, an 'artificial' way of classifying plants. The first of its 26 parts was published in 1759 with Bute agreeing to underwrite its entire publication to avoid financial risk to Hill. This work took 16 years to complete with 1,600 plates drawn by Hill.

Bute commissioned botanical artists to record flowers for both his and the royal collection. Simon Taylor was first employed at 17 to paint rare plants in 1760, having trained with William Shipley, founder of the Society of Arts. He produced at least 68 illustrations on vellum for Bute and numerous drawings. Taylor did not, however, achieve the brilliance of George Ehret, a distinguished flower painter from Heidelberg, who had made early illustrations for Linnaeus. After settling in London he was patronised by wealthy clients and could charge 1 guinea per vellum. Bute commissioned 131 watercolours from him. John Miller, another illustrator for Linnaeus, painted 956 watercolours in six volumes for Bute, and John Edwards made 232. Most of these images were dispersed when Bute's natural history library was sold in 1794. Yet others artists were encouraged by Bute: Margaret Meen, who exhibited at the Royal Academy from 1775 onwards and published a periodical *Exotic Plants from the Royal Gardens at Kew*, and the newly widowed Mrs Delany, a friend of Lady Bute. Her exquisite paper collages, some of specimens from Kew, are now lodged in the British Museum.

While the gardens at Kew were flourishing Bute, became Ranger of Richmond Park and introduced Lancelot 'Capability' Brown to the King. This led to Brown's appointment as Master Gardener at Hampton Court with responsibility for the gardens at Richmond in 1764. Brown worked simultaneously for Bute at Luton and the King at Richmond. It is probable that Bute would have had an input in the gardens at Richmond. Brown assuredly had an involvement at Kew because in 1767 he wrote to Bute apologising that certain trees had not been planted correctly there.

The King and his family came to Richmond Lodge for a long summer stay in 1764 following which Brown produced a plan for the re-development of the gardens. With the help of his foreman, Michael Milliken, from Chatsworth, Brown swept away Bridgeman's canal and ponds, the long riverside terrace walk, Kent's buildings with the exception of the Hermitage, which was left as a ruin, and the small village of West Sheen. The grass now undulated down to the river and, though many visitors missed the terrace, devotees of the Picturesque Movement like Uvedale Price felt that it was a great improvement. The woods were thinned out, leaving small clumps and single trees to give a more informal and natural-looking landscape. The Royal Observatory, designed by Chambers, was built in the south of the estate to record the transit of Venus across the sun in 1769. Chambers was particularly vitriolic about Brown's improvements, which may have been related to disappointment at the lack of progress of his own project for

the King. With no single house at Kew or Richmond large enough to accommodate the royal family, the King wanted to replace Richmond Lodge, no longer considered a suitable royal residence, with a new abode. In 1765 Chambers produced the first of a number of plans for a magnificent palace within the grounds, of which only one was ever begun but never completed.

Many scurrilous political cartoons had been directed at Bute but the publication of *Lord Bute's Erections*, in 1767, a cartoon suggesting an affair with Princess Augusta, proved too offensive for him. It implied that he would sneak out of his back gate, erroneously depicted at on the illustration, to dally with her in the gardens at Kew. The following year he departed for Europe while Princess Augusta spent less and less time at Kew, only coming from London in summer twice a week to breakfast with her elder children. On her death in 1772 Kew reverted to the King who moved into the White House shortly afterwards and demolished Richmond

Lord Bute's Erections a cartoon in the *Political Register*, 1767. L marks Bute's back gate through which it was alleged he could tryst with Princess Augusta.

Lodge. With Bute now completely out of favour, Joseph Banks, recently returned from his plant-hunting expedition accompanying Captain Cook around the world, was appointed Kew's director the following year to inject his youthful enthusiasm and drive into expanding the botanical collections. Bute gave up the lease on his house on Kew Green and, though continuing his correspondence with Queen Charlotte, retired to Luton and ultimately Highcliffe.

Queen Charlotte took a keen interest in the continuing expansion and development of both the royal gardens. A cottage *orné*, named for her and which still stands today, was put up on the site of Queen Caroline's menagerie at Richmond. The King's attention, however, was diverted to Windsor Castle where he indulged in farming and hunting. The public were now permitted to visit all of Richmond Gardens on Sunday and Kew on Thursday, often causing a

jam of carriages on Kew Green. The White House was demolished in 1802 in the same year that the flanking walls of Love Lane, though closed for public use since 1785, were eventually taken down to unite the two estates. In 1840 William Hooker was appointed director of Kew and the estate freed from royal ownership to allow it independence.

White House, 1763.

In 1784 Bute published his great treatise *Botanical Tables*, illustrated by John Miller with 654 plates and dedicated to Queen Charlotte. In addition to the nine volumes, he presented her with a small satinwood cabinet for housing them, its doors painted with flowers including a red martagon lily, a white rose and a passion flower. These were bought, after her death, by her eldest son and remain within the royal collection. The Tables, which had occupied Bute for many years, were intended as a way of identifying British flora using keys he had devised and were specially designed for women, written in English rather than Latin. It was neither a new way of classifying flora nor a riposte to Linnaeus as some claim. According to Dr Nigel Taylor, the former curator of horticulture at Kew, they form a remarkable piece of work of which more copies should have been made at the time. However, they did cost Bute

Box given by 3rd
Earl of Bute to
Queen Charlotte in
which to store the
Botanical Tables.

£10,000 to produce a limited print run of 12 sets. His daughter Lady Macartney, his sister-in-law Lady Betty Mackenzie, the Empress of Russia and the Duchess of Portland were all given copies. Unlike Linnaeus, who refused his daughters an education in science, Bute believed in the importance of education for women and Queen Charlotte, under his influence, made sure that her own six daughters all received lessons in botany and flower painting, with both the Princesses Charlotte and Elizabeth showing particular talent. As with Mrs Delany, botanical accuracy in recording the correct number of flower parts was considered important in their work and it is known that John Miller's illustrations were used as aides memoires.

The 3rd Earl of Bute has never been properly credited with the creation of Kew, arguably the finest botanic garden in the world and model for many others. The contribution of Sir Joseph Banks has, in many ways, masked Bute's initial impact. It was his systematic and scientific methodology from the beginning, and his appointment of and delegation to talented people, which allowed the gardens to take off and expand into what they have become today. His *Botanical Tables* have long lain forgotten and unread but attest to his energy and knowledge and, perhaps most of all, his ability to impart this knowledge to others. With more political adroitness he might have been acknowledged as a renowned scientist, first director of Kew and sincere Prime Minister and given more credit within his lifetime. It is ironic that he has had to wait for more than 200 years for due appreciation.

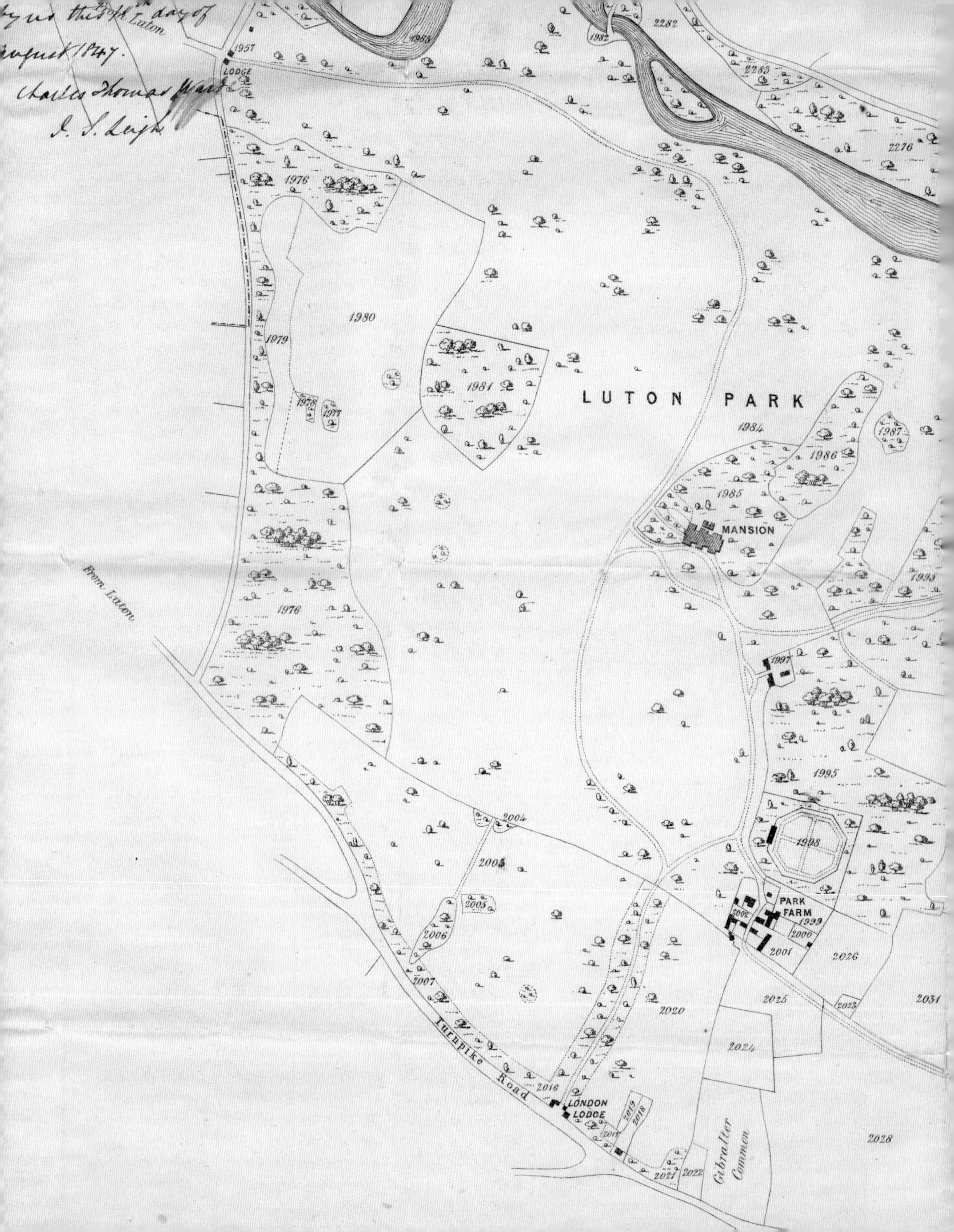

By me this 30th day of
August 1847.
Charles Thomas Hurst
J. S. Leigh

LODGE
1957
1955
1982
2282
2283
2276
1976
1980
1979
1981
LUTON PARK
1984
1987
1986
1985
MANSION
1978
1977
1993
From Luton
1976
1997
1995
2004
2005
1998
2005
PARK FARM
1999
2006
2008
2000
2007
2001
2026
2020
2025
2023
2031
Turnpike Road
2016
2024
LONDON LODGE
2019
2018
2017
2021
2022
Gibralter Common
2028

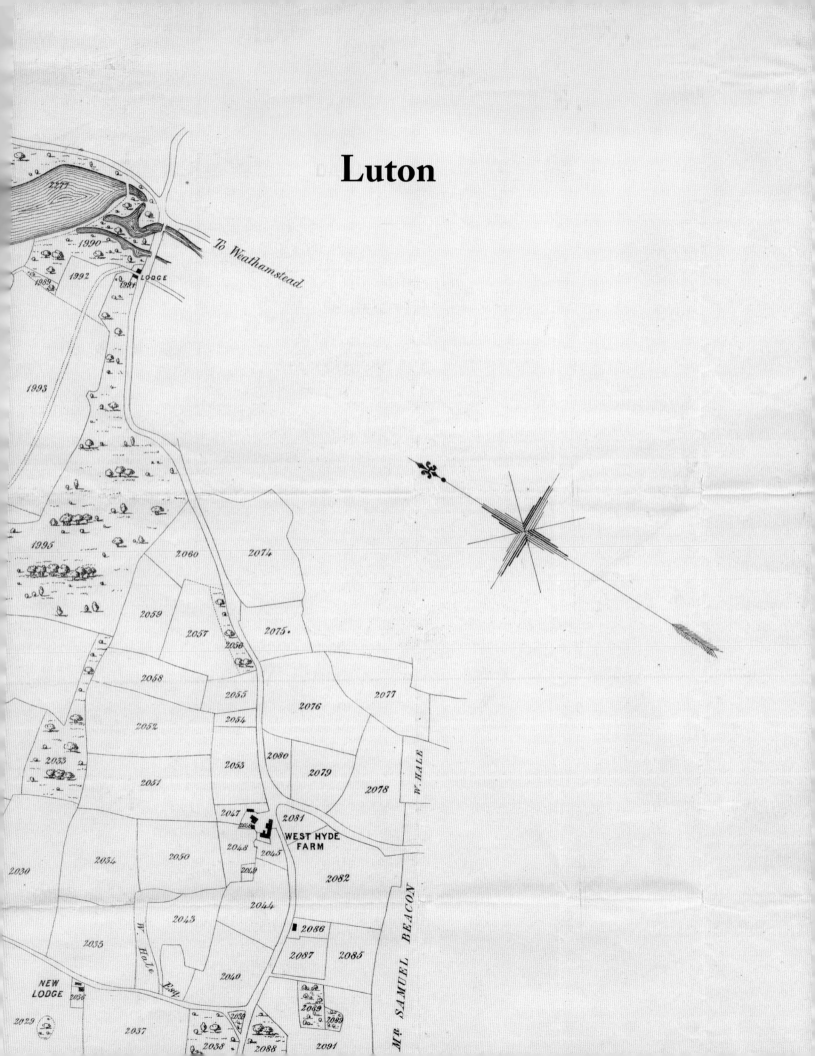

Luton

2271

1990

To Wealhamstead

1989 1992 1991 LODGE

1993

1995

2060 2074

2059

2057 2056 2075

2058

2055 2076 2077

2052 2054

2033 2080 2079

2051 2053 2078 W. HALE

2047 2081

2030 2034 2050 2048 WEST HYDE FARM 2045 2049 2082

2044 Mr SAMUEL BEACON

2043 W. Hole Esq. 2086

2035 2087 2085

NEW LODGE 2036

2029 2040

2037 2089 2089

2038 2088 2091

Luton Hoo, on the southern borders of Bedfordshire, 29 miles north of London, was part of an ancient manor, originally owned by the Hoo family in the eleventh century. A late sixteenth century house of redbrick, facing south-west, around which was enclosed 300 acres of parkland, was built for Sir Robert Napier, ennobled by James I. The estate subsequently passed from Frances Napier to her nephew, Francis Herne MP, from whom John, the 3rd Earl of Bute, bought it in 1763 for £94,700. Another 1,000 acres of adjoining farmland were purchased at the same time. The objects of this country residence were to create a garden to satisfy his appetite for plant collecting and an enormous library for his botanical books. It was to become a haven of safety where a by now disgraced ex-Prime Minister could escape the jostling crowds of London and the lampooning of the press. Under the Butes it was called Luton Park, dropping the ancient postfix Hoo, to which it has since reverted.

Old house at
Luton in 1763,
by Paul Sandby.

Not satisfied with the house as they found it and benefiting from the vast fortune left by Lady Bute's father who had died in 1761, the Butes commissioned Lancelot Brown to improve the parkland as a setting for a magnificent new mansion. Robert Adam, designer of the Butes' town house near Berkeley Square in London's Mayfair, was chosen as architect with the brief to accommodate Bute's large family and his ever-increasing library. After countless amendments to the plan, agreement was finally reached in 1767 and the building programme begun. The first stage proceeded with ranges to the east and south and took six years. So constant was the dialogue between client and architect that in the preface to his book, *Works*, Adam acknowledged Bute's "great taste and discerning judgement in the celebrated works of the ancients, and in every branch of the fine arts". The old house remained as the new was being built around it. They were still connected when Mrs Delany visited in 1774, the entrance

DAUGHTERS of JOHN 3RD EARL of BUTE.

Daughters of 3rd
Earl at Luton by
Johann Zoffany,
1764.

to the new being through the old house. The second stage of building was abandoned for the
time being and only completed 50 years later.

Bute had introduced 'Capability' Brown to George III when he was prime minister.
The King had looked at the amendments to Kensington Palace grounds that Brown was
planning in 1762, and two years later appointed him "Surveyor to his Majesty's Gardens and
Waters at Hampton Court." Brown may well have informed Bute of the impending sale of
the Luton estate where it is thought that in 1756 he had carried out planting as well as the
construction of the column, north Gatehouse and a Palladian arch for Francis Herne.

Johann Zoffany painted a charming portrait of three of the Butes' daughters
beside that Palladian arch in 1763 and a paired portrait of their three younger sons under
a tree. At the same time Bute commissioned a series of watercolours and gouaches of the
estate from Paul Sandby, introduced to him by his close friend, Lord Harcourt of Nuneham
Courtney, who was both patron and pupil of the artist. They were painted during the first
years of his ownership and show a landscape of some maturity before Brown embarked on
any of his changes. Subjects include a fine beech-lined drive, good plantings of oak and ash
with specimen birches and new round clumps planted with conifers, so typical of his style of
improvement, possibly as nurse trees for Brown's preferred deciduous species. Horned cattle

THE ARCHBISHOP OF ARMAGH AND BROTHERS WHEN BOYS.

Sons of the 3rd Earl at Luton by Johann Zoffany, 1764.

and fallow deer graze the park in between the clumps and horses roam freely. The picturesque is featured in a venerable beech hosting bracket fungus and an old, ivy-covered gate lodge standing alone in open landscape to the west of the house.

The start of Brown's landscaping by October 1764 preceded work on the house. A curved sunken fence or ha-ha, following the contours of the land for unimpeded views from the house to the south and east, ran through two existing groves, which were densely planted up to disguise the ditch and soften its impact when seen from the other side. There was a path through an opening to the south-east and, further along the ha-ha, was a viewpoint out over the River Lee at the end of a wide gravel path. Another gravel path led out from the south of the house and skirted an oval lawn for which a sundial and a hexagonal stone table were planned. The lawn continued down a valley south to where Brown's plan shows two mature trees near the ha-ha, one with a seat around it to look out over the vista. It also shows seven island beds of shrubs and small trees providing variety to the lawns. A gravel walk through a mature wood looped around an old quarry where a seat was placed to take advantage of sloping ground and command magnificent views over the River Lee. A still surviving cedar indicates its position. To frame a view from the east of the house to the river, already being widened into a lake, Brown planted on both sides of an

ample lawn a variety of trees, which certainly included some purple beeches, known to be growing at Kew in 1766, and some still-standing cedars. Amongst these groups he placed a second seat around a mature tree. To the north of the house a stand of well-spaced and stately Cedar of Lebanon, *Cedrus libani*, remain from this time. Though his client had vision and determination, the success of the landscaping at Luton can safely be attributed to Brown's characteristic planting genius.

At least 20 years previously, at Mount Stuart, Bute had had sea water pumped up to the house to take bracing baths for his health so his request for water to be piped up to Luton House and for flushing toilets there should not be see as exceptional for the time. Robert Adam, moreover, had specified toilets and piped water in his designs for Dumfries House 10 years before although such a supply had been gravity fed, but at Luton a more sophisticated engineering system was needed to raise water from the River Lee. Arguably Brown's hydraulic competence in draining, damming and supplying water for other landed clients may have been as significant as his landscaping skills in earning him the Luton commission. Bute was, after all, an accomplished gardener with experience at planting at Mount Stuart, Kew and Kenwood House. Furthermore, Brown is known to have made drawings of the wings of the house where the water closets were to be located. In addition to the needs of the house, a lot of water would be needed for the botanic garden. A bore-hole was sunk in Engine Wood to be the source of much of its supply.

Plan for landscaped garden, including part of the house, sundial, stone table, Dell plantation, Seat, Gravel Walk, and sunk fence, c. 1764, ink and wash, Lancelot 'Capability' Brown (1716–1783).

Brown started by damming the winding River Lee in two places to create a pair of curved, elongated lakes a mile long, with an island in the lower one emerging from previously wooded rising ground. A cascade with a ten foot drop gushed over the upper dam and was crossed by a brick bridge. A plan, by Brown, has recently been identified as very likely the design for the construction of this part of the lake. The water flowed over the substantial lower dam to the south in a sheer drop of 30 feet. To its north over the narrowest part of the lake a wooden bridge connected to a walk along the east bank and a gravel drive westwards up to the house. By the summer of 1765 the lakes were beginning to fill up, but took 13 years to reach their final spread of 50 acres, indicating the problems that Brown had in their development and reflecting his bill of over £12,000. This was Brown's second most expensive commission after that of Blenheim. Two boats and a sloop moored on the lake were constructed from estate timber, to be joined later by at least three boathouses.

Gentlemen conversing on a drive at Luton by Paul Sandby, c. 1763. This illustrates how Brown was often required to 'improve' already mature landscapes.

Brown planted up the far side of the lake with a mixture of lime, horse chestnut, oak and beech, scattered with conifers and some poplars. To draw the eye up the valley from the south and to balance the trees on the island, a purple beech, just newly introduced to England from Germany, was probably planted at this time. It may be the one which survives today with its lower branches touching the ground and enveloping a glowing ruby cabinet beneath its canopy. The north entrance drive sweeping past the purple beech up to the house was designed to maximise views over the lake while new planting and the belt of mature beeches through which it passed hid the house from sight until just before the point of arrival.

In 1765 Bute escaped again to Luton where he spent the whole summer quietly with his son, Mountstuart, who was newly returned from the Continent. He began to think of travelling abroad himself but meanwhile continued to collect folios of flower paintings and prints, books and scientific instruments. Although Brown drew up a plan for a rectangular walled garden beside the lake near the lower cascade, Bute must have decided that the local source of water did not justify such a distance from the house. An unusual octagonal walled garden, credited to Brown and still intact, along with Bute's botanical collection and Flower Garden Wood were laid out on higher ground to the south of the house, beyond Adam's intended stable block. The rejected piece of land by the lake was planted up with yew, box and oak as probable shrubberies to a pleasure garden near a boat house and to screen the engine house which has since been rebuilt. However, the glorious concept of the Flower Garden Wood next to the walled garden may well have been Bute's, knowing his planting programme for Mount Stuart and his exacting requirements. Brown's deference to his client shows in a letter responding to one of rebuke for the method of tree planting under his care at Kew in 1767.

Kew was used as a source for the plants at Luton. Brown writes: "We have got as many trees as we wanted this season from the Princess of Wales' garden, on which acct.

Deer, horses and cattle graze around ivy-clad ruins, with the Napier Column in the lefthand distance. Paul Sandby, c. 1763.

I desired Mr Haverfield to forward the trees for your Lordship as fast as possible." Some of these may also have come from Whitton, the garden of Bute's late uncle, the 3rd Duke of Argyll. Brown's foreman, William Ireland, was in charge of tree planting at Luton and evidence remains even today of the transplanting of mature trees with branches pruned back to ensure that the trees survived. A remarkable horse chestnut stands guarding the lower cascade and there are grafted cedars and lime trees from this period indicating that some horticultural experimentation was being carried out.

George III still relied on Bute's advice although he no longer held political office. In an audience with the King before leaving London in 1765, Bute had explained that, due to his own unpopularity, he felt unable to be of any more use to his majesty and that he would go abroad if it would make matters easier. The King took time to accept this but within two years had turned completely against Bute, who then became very ill and was urged by friends to travel on the Continent. He sailed from England in August 1768 accompanied by his favourite son, Charles. The Countess was left with the job of coordinating building works at Luton and paying the bills during his absence. While collecting pictures, vases, statues and furnishings and commissioning

View north along the lake to a purple beech in 2007.

marble fireplaces to be sent to England, Bute dispatched frequent letters home with ideas for Luton. Dr John Symmonds, a fellow traveller in Italy, reported to him from there in 1770 "the kitchen garden actually looked as if it had been planted 2 years", despite its very recent creation.

Returning to England in May 1771 he rushed to Luton to see the progress achieved there. He found that Brown had banished fallow deer from the park, probably to protect the newly planted exotics in the woods, including *Rhododendron ponticum*, only just introduced to Britain from around the Black Sea, and *R. maximum* from North America. Bute settled down to a reclusive life there, managing his library and ordering new flower prints from the continent. He would allow visits, though, from certain scientific colleagues and exchange plants with others such as Professor Marsili at Padua Botanic Garden. The Countess and their unmarried daughter, Louisa, would usually come in July, after the London season, staying until the autumn "trailing to the farm and dawdling to the flower garden". The family would retire to the library after tea until the supper bell. Such was their desire for privacy that Horace Walpole was denied admittance when he tried to call on them in 1772. Later that year following the death of Princess Augusta, George III's mother, whose gardens he had helped to create at Kew, Bute dedicated to her memory the Napier Column, a tall stone Tuscan pillar at Luton, replacing its urn with a figure of a robed woman.

A conservatory built in 1775 in the kitchen garden, described as "the most perfect in the kingdom", was 195 feet long and divided into three equal sections. Probably designed by Brown, who stayed with Bute at Luton that year, but drawn by Robert Nasmith who submitted

Collage of *Fumaria vesicaria* by Mrs Delany on 21 June 1778.

other drawings of greenhouses, it was filled with exotics. Lady Mary Coke, Bute's cousin, reported that: "those plants which not at all times bear the natural air have Houses of such extent as amazed me." Mrs Delany, a friend of Lady Bute, selected flowers from Luton with which to make some of her collages, now in the British Museum. These give an indication of the range of plants Bute was growing in his collection at Luton. Many plants originated in Africa: *Fumaria vesicaria*, a delicate white climber, and *Lotus arabicus* with its pink flower both from the north of the continent; the dark red *Erica cerinthoides*, a heather, and *Agapanthus umbellatus* from its southern tip. Bute was also known to be growing *Camellia japonica* under glass since it was not until 1814 that *Curtis' Botanical magazine* first wrote that outside cultivation was possible in Britain. Mrs Delany's camellia collage made in December 1779 was from one of his specimens. Two years before it is credited with having been introduced to Britain, was another plant of note recorded in 1778, *Cistus formosus* from Portugal, now known as *Halimium lasianthum*, with its vibrant coloured flowers.

By 1783 there were ten to twelve gardeners under two head gardeners, one employed exclusively in the kitchen garden and pinery, the other in charge of the grounds and shrubberies. There was a rock garden, probably in the old quarry, along with aquatic plants and a bog area. By now, Bute's Flower Garden Wood and his botanical collection in four acres were well established with their own catalogue, the plants named according to the Linnaean system and in both Latin and English to aid students. The botanic garden was probably laid out in a similar way to that at Kew with a central path and order beds to each side. An article in

the *General Evening Post* praised the library as being second only to Blenheim in the whole of Europe and said of the garden: "Excepting the king's residence at Kew, a botanical garden is an appendage peculiar to this place; and his lordship, with a liberal seal for science, has given orders that it is to be open to all comers."

View of Luton over the river with a cart by Charles Steuart, 1775.

However, it was Lady Mary Coke, who summed up the glory of Luton's flower gardens:

... the quantity of flowers is amazing... I believe there is thirty acres of ground laid out in walks with a boarder (sic) for flowers of twelve feet on each side which is now in its high beauty as the flowers now bloming (sic) are almost all of them sweet & they perfume the air. There is a flower garden besides which is for those of a superior kind in short there is nothing like it... which you will easily believe when you consider that Ld Bute understands all these things beyond any other Person & that he spares no expense.

As the Butes grew older life at Luton became less attractive. The Countess developed gout in 1783 and found walking increasingly difficult which, along with his own poor health, may have precipitated Bute's decision to retire to Highcliffe the following September. He lost interest in completing the house, which no longer appealed to any of the family despite his son William becoming Rector of Luton in 1779. Louisa speaks of the "intolerable yawnings" of the gatherings there and gladly escaped with her father to the less sophisticated and more isolated life of Highcliffe. Bute closed the pinery but had the garden with its exotics and the park kept up.

When the 3rd Earl died in 1792, Luton and its contents were left in his will to Lord Mountstuart, his heir. The capital and income enjoyed by Bute through his wife was not available to the new Earl as her wealth was to be settled on his brother, James. The provision of £4,000 to each of two of his brothers and his unmarried sister, Louisa, depleted the resources of the new owner. He immediately let out the park at Luton for twenty one years and sold off the livestock. After his wife Charlotte died in 1800 he quickly married Fanny Coutts, the daughter of the London banker. Her fortune of £100,000 alleviated his financial problems but in the meantime the conservatory had been dismantled and Louisa reported that the botanic garden had become overgrown, perhaps exacerbated by a severe storm in November 1795 which caused considerable damage. With the new century repairs were undertaken and new trees planted along with some clearing and restocking in the Flower Garden Wood. The icehouse was thatched and work carried out on the pump in Engine Spring Wood.

When John, the 2nd Marquess, inherited in 1814, the estate was valued at £200,000. He initially decided to make Luton the centre of administration of his English and Welsh estates, appointing Thomas Collingdon as his secretary to be resident there. However, being the only one of his five properties which had not been in his family for long, he felt less attachment to it when deciding to rationalise his affairs and he put Luton up for sale. In 1821 he wrote: "If I sell... within £20,000 of the valuation I should after establishing my library and pictures at Mount Stuart or Cardiff... have as large a landed income as at this moment."

By 1824 with no suitable buyers, he took it off the market and the following year employed Robert Smirke, architect of the British Museum, to finish off Robert Adam's grand scheme. Smirke demolished the seventeenth century house and built new north and west ranges each with an Ionic portico. The work was finished by 1830 when Henry Shaw's folio of drawings of the chapel was published, showing the incorporation of late-Medieval woodwork from the old house. A new conservatory was built along the north-west wall of the walled garden although at a time when the Marquess so rarely resided at Luton. Brown's simple plunging cascade was replaced with a five-stepped stone structure at the outlet of the lake and an iron bridge was ordered from Barnwell and Hagger in 1830, to replace Brown's wooden one, at a total cost of £475. Lady Bute's lodge on the southern boundary of the park near

West Hyde Farm was probably built soon after in the neo-Gothic style using part of an old Norman arch, in honour of Maria North, the Marquess' first wife.

On 8th November, 1843, the under-gardener, James Lines, discovered that the house was on fire. The cause was related to work plumbers had been doing on the copper roof above the hall. Mrs Partridge, the housekeeper, was alerted and organised the servants to rescue 40,000 books from the 146 feet long library and the most valuable paintings from throughout the house, thereby saving a large part of the 3rd Earl's artistic legacy. The hall, chapel and library were destroyed as the fire engines were starved of sufficient water when the pumps powering the supply broke down. Two years previously Maria, John's wife, had died without issue, and her Cambridgeshire estates reverted to the North family. With fewer reasons to live in that part of England, John's interest in Luton again waned and he succeeded in selling it in 1845.

In 1848 it was sold on to a Liverpool lawyer, John Shaw Leigh, who at once set about reconstructing the house with Sydney Smirke, Robert's younger brother, as the architect. New greenhouses and lighted frames were constructed within and around the walled kitchen garden and the Old Park Farm buildings to the south were demolished, a new 'state of the art' model farm being built in their place, designed by George Halton. Considerable enlargements were made to the Adam stables. However, it was his son, John Gerard Leigh, who had the house completed, and a new chapel built to the design of GE Street, after his marriage in 1872 to Mrs Eleanor Dudley Ward, a close friend of the Prince of Wales. For the rest of the century the house played stage to her glamorous social life and a skating rink was dug to the east of the house within Brown's 1764 landscape.

1817 print of Luton Park with ha-ha.

Leigh managed the estate to maximise its potential for field sports in which he was so interested. In 1855 the lake was well stocked with fish and reportedly covered with swans, wild geese, ducks, coots, moorhens and other fowl. A small footbridge crossed to the island, east of which the river meander silted up, creating a marsh hospitable to birds. He also built a pheasantry and kennels near the lower cascade. However, the laying of the Midland and Great Northern railway to the east of the lake, completed in 1868, led to an alteration in the park boundaries. With the road diverted south, the old east lodges near the cascade were replaced by a new pair of lodges at each side of heavy iron gates erected immediately east of the iron bridge at the bottom of the lake, connecting directly with the road to Luton.

Sir Julius Wernher, the diamond magnate, rented the house for a few years following the death of Mrs Leigh. In 1903 he bought the estate and set about completely remodelling the interior in the *belle époque* style as a backdrop to his art collection, using Charles Mewès and Arthur Davis, architects of the Ritz Hotel in London. It was at this time that the mansard roof was added to Luton for more staff accommodation. An Italian garden with fountain and a pair of small pavilions was laid out by WH Romaine Walker to the south of the house on Brown's lawn. Soon followed a Japanese garden in the old quarry, the planting of a wellingtonia avenue, and the arboretum, begun in 1895, was extended into the pleasure grounds. An elaborate conservatory and set of glasshouses were constructed by the firm of Mackenzie and Moncur in the walled garden reintroducing tropical plants to Luton Hoo.

South lawn and house framed by the 'Capability' Brown tree plantings in 2006.

During the Second World War the estate was requisitioned by the Army, following which Sir Julius' son, Harold, with his wife, Anastasia, daughter of Grand Duke Michael of Russia, commissioned Philip Tilden to make alterations to the house. These were intended to better display their art collection, enhanced by the addition of Russian artefacts, part of the Romanov inheritance. The house was opened to the public in May 1950.

The house and the greater portion of the pleasure grounds and park but not the walled garden and farm were sold by Wernher descendents in 1999 to Elite hotels. They have undertaken a major restoration and reorganisation of the estate. Accommodation for both staff and guests, along with a swimming pool, has been erected in the Flower Garden Wood next to the Adam stables. The main hotel opened after refurbishment in September 2007. Warren Weir, a conference centre for 200 delegates with 81 bedrooms has been constructed near the lower cascade. The walled garden and its impressive range of glass buildings form part of a separate research and restoration project.

Noise levels from Luton airport nearby may be irreducible but the orange-coloured hangar on the brow of the hill to the north-east would intrude less if painted a more subdued tone. Despite the many alterations to the buildings and environmental changes to the landscape beyond and recently within, the house in its setting overlooking the valley and lake still remains a testimony to the days of the 3rd Earl and the skill of his professional and artistic advisers, Robert Adam and Lancelot 'Capability' Brown.

Looking over the south lawn to the lake from the house in 2006.

Highcliffe

While on a plant hunting expedition to the New Forest, the 3rd Earl of Bute was first attracted to the isolated location of Highcliffe where, in 1775, he built "a cottage for the Sea Air and bathing". The site yielded fossils in its cliffs, several rare plants in the locality, and a sweeping view south-east across Christchurch Bay to the Isle of Wight with its dentate promontory, The Needles. Looking south across the turf of a well drained friable soil underlain by gravel lay the expanse of the English Channel. To the west stood the silhouettes of Christchurch Priory and the tower surmounting Hengistbury Head with the Purbeck Hills beyond, suitable eye-catchers to be borrowed for his personal landscape. Not only would the sea-air temper the climate to suit his experiments in growing exotic plants but it was also known to be therapeutic. His surgeon, Sir William Fordyce, built his own house, Belvedere, slightly inland of Highcliffe. Moreover, the slope of the cliff allowed stepped walks to be made to the shore with the possibility of sea bathing, favoured by Bute. Though remote, access from the main road which ran from Lymington to Christchurch parallel to the coast was easy. Perhaps, too, its cliff-top position and views onto another hilly shore across a stretch of water comparable in width to the Firth of Clyde recalled the home of his young adulthood, Mount Stuart.

High Cliff (as the 3rd Earl's house was known) from the east by Charles Steuart, c. 1775. Workmen are repairing the cliff top path in the foreground. Hengistbury Head looms in the distance.

The known disadvantages of this site included the strong prevailing winds from the south-west which dictated the low and massy form which the house was to take, unprotected at the outset by any shelter from trees. More disturbing was the instability of the cliff upon which the house was built as described by a near neighbour, the Rev. William Gilpin:

Previous pages: The path to the beach down the unconsolidated sea cliff. The kiosk attributed to 'Capability' Brown appears on the right while the roofs of a rotunda and temple can just be seen above the cliff-line.

> The cliff... is about fifty, or sixty yards high. It is not perpendicular, but the ground being of a spongy, foundering nature, is continually falling in huge masses.... Within these last twenty years the sea has gained near a

quarter of a mile, in some places on this coast; and the calculators of the country say that Lord Bute's house cannot possibly stand above thirty years. He has taken however great pains to secure it, by diverting, at a great expense, the land springs: so that he has little to fear but the action of the sea which, though a rough enemy, is a much less dangerous one; and against this he has endeavoured to guard by facing the precipice in different parts with stone.

High Cliff from the west by Charles Steuart, c. 1775. In the distance can be seen The Needles on the Isle of Wight.

The house began with two stories above a semi-basement and a four bay facade, flanked by three storied towers lit by bow windows looking onto the sea. It was aligned at a slight north-westerly angle to the cliff line and only some 60 metres from its edge. Although its design has traditionally been attributed to Robert Adam, Robert Nasmith, who had worked at Luton, superintended the extensive additions that were to follow and is likely to have been involved from the beginning. Bute might have had the skills to prepare the designs for it but needed a professional to oversee the work. Payments were made from Bute's accounts to the building company of the Adam family, but not one drawing of Highcliffe appears in the Adam archives. In 1778 a short wing was added to each side, extended by projecting bowed end bays with paired windows to benefit from the views. They were flanked by free-standing, pedimented pavilions connected by a wall with blind arcades. In 1783 another wing was built by eliminating the projecting side bows. This was as Charles Steuart painted it from a point just south of west. The four bowed projections appear like towers. There are no analogous bowed towers in any of Adam's authenticated classical works, challenging the tradition that Highcliffe was designed by him.

The project was pursued without the support or interest of Lady Bute but she condescended to praise its views and compared its rooms rather favourably with those of Luton when she at last visited in 1779. Her gouty frame had fewer steps to climb upstairs. In her words: "The mildness of the sea air... makes up for the want of shelter, there not being a single tree upon our territory." The act of building his house before landscaping is a curious reversal of Bute's process at Luton. This may indicate his growing enchantment with Highcliffe and its future role for a botanic collection. It should not be overlooked that Lancelot Brown had already been consulted, with payments recorded in his ledgers for work in 1777 and 1778 but the nature of his involvement at Highcliffe is unclear since Bute was paying for Luton at the same time.

Steuart's paintings show the Brownian idyll of turf lapping the facade of the house with the sward extending to the cliff edge. In one painting the grass is being tended by a gardener leading a horse yoked to a roller; in the other, workmen are repairing the cliff-top path. Another path leads from the central door out of the dining room towards the west where shrubs were arranged in clumps. To the east of the house is an extended line of wind-shorn trees and shrubs, beyond which stands a rotunda and further along the cliff a temple with pedimented portico. These are mirrored by a pair of identical structures to the west. By about 1786 trees had grown sufficiently to frame the westerly temple while the adjacent rotunda was left in dramatic isolation to silhouette against the seascape. An octagonal kiosk of chinoiserie charm stood at the top of a stepped walkway from the beach in front of the house. This is assumed to be the bathing place mentioned in Humphry Repton's list of Brown's works, further confirming his contribution to Highcliffe.

To protect the garden behind the house from the prevailing winds ran a brick wall to the north-west. Reinforcing its purpose was a plantation of pines whose value was utilitarian in view of their speed of growth and tolerance to sandy soils and maritime conditions. The Maritime pine *Pinus pinaster* later became known as the Bournemouth pine, due to its extensive use along the stretch of coast west from Christchurch in the nineteenth century, and Bute used conifers as nurse trees in his other landscapes. There is good reason to believe that the flower garden was laid out in a walled enclosure and most of the shrubberies and stands of exotic trees planted in the lee of this wall and of the shelter of massed conifers.

Tender plants grew in four glazed houses in the flower garden, two of 60 feet length and two of 25 feet length, although the sales catalogue for the house mentioned a "capital conservatory near 250 feet long... with an Observatory in the middle". Plants in the "long west conservatory" included various succulents of African and American origin, a wide range of Mediterranean plants and from temperate South America what Bute's great-granddaughter considered to have been the first successful fuchsia grown in England, *F. coccinea*, although it is known that this species arrived at Kew by 1789. The *Camellia japonica* from China, illustrated by Mrs Delany from Bute's collection, was also under glass and, like the fuchsia, did not need such protection. Several of the glass houses accommodated myrtles and mimosas "of Botany Bay" and two varieties of banksias, *B. ericifolia* and *B. dentata*, which must have caused a sensation. Plants from Australia had only started to be introduced from 1770 following the discovery of that continent; the banksias just from 1788. That these plants were so soon growing at Highcliffe shows the regard held for Bute by Joseph Banks, Kew's director.

Supplementing the houses were "reed hedge inclosures" where more "green house plants" were sheltered outside. These had origins in southern Europe and the tropical and warm temperate parts of the Americas, Africa and Asia, but also included an Australian plant, the dusky coral pea *Kennedia rubicunda*, identified in the catalogue under its previous name *Glycine rubicunda*. Another "reed hedge inclosure" accommodated mainly American plants in pots or baskets such as andromedas, kalmias and *Magnolia acuminata*, although it was presumably being used as a holding area pending their planting out since such American plants were also growing in the ground. It is conventional and reasonable to assume that many plants were transferred from Luton to Highcliffe.

High Cliff from the sea by Adam Callander, late eighteenth century. The pair of rotundas and temples is visible on each side of the house.

89

Camelia japonica
collage by Mrs
Delany on 20
December 1779.

What was "planted in the earth" in those "Patches of the most costly Exotics and other Herbaceous Plants" included well over 100 species, identified by copper labels with their Linnaean names. 400 laurels, both Portuguese *Prunus lusitanica* and "common laurels" *Prunus laurocerasus* would have afforded shelter to the more decorative North American species such as summersweet *Clethra alnifolia*, buttonbush *Cephalanthus occidentalis* and Carolina allspice *Calycanthus floridus* as well as the distinctly dangerous poison ivy *Rhus toxicodendron* and poison sumach *Rhus vernix*. Other European shrubs Bute used included sea buckthorn *Rhamnus alaternus*, phillyrea and *Viburnum tinus*. The specimen trees he planted were largely from North America: catalpas, tulip trees, liquidambars, gleditsias and, amongst the conifers, Chinese arbour-vitae *Thuja orientalis* and a single Weymouth pine *Pinus strobus* with plenty of junipers, the most commonly used being the pencil cedar *Juniperus virginiana*. Strawberry trees were favoured, both *Arbutus unedo*, native to Ireland, and *A. andrachne* from Cyprus. Rhododendrons *R. ponticum* from Eurasia and *R. ferrugineum* from the Alps seem strange geographical bedfellows with azaleas and other plants from North America in a large circle dedicated to plants of American origin. Two other circles were filled with over 100 shrubs and herbaceous plants from no specific area of the world.

In addition, the "long kitchen garden" grew over 200 fruit trees comprising a wide variety of apples, apricots, cherries, nectarines, peaches, pears and plums. Another 50 fruit trees were planted in the "rasberry quarter", and 60 more were trained up against 'the wall' where they were grown behind herbaceous plants and low shrubs and inter-planted with a variety of climbers. There were ornamental plants in another kitchen garden.

The final extensions to the house, symmetrically arranged as with all previous additions, were three bays wide by nine bays deep, extending back to give shelter to the coach-turning circle and principal entrance. They were completed in 1788. In the new west wing were four libraries on two floors housing many of Lord Bute's collection of books brought from Luton which, when sold in 1794, needed several days of auction. Under the libraries were housed his laboratory with "Materia Medica", his forge and collection of fossils and minerals which together required two days to sell in August 1795. The east wing was for servants' accommodation and kitchens. Within the completed house were 19 bedrooms for guests and 13 for servants, several water closets and a two-storey saloon. It was a massive denial of its 'cottage' origins. A caller, who never saw beyond this side of the building, wrote, with perhaps a touch of petulance at being denied access: "Its back front is what is generally termed superb— to us however it appeared a confusion of building, without elegance."

The constant additions reflect Bute's passion for Highcliffe and the need to be surrounded by his accumulating collections and, on occasions, his friends and family. It is known that he spent almost four months there without company in 1785, its isolation affording him the opportunity to concentrate on preparing his oeuvre *Botanical Tables, containing the different Family's of British Plants*. The erosion of the cliffs must have been of concern to him if he did take the action reported by Gilpin. However, it might not have worried him as much as it should have since its menace was disguised by his head gardener, Ross, who was always anxious to "turn a walk and turf it over before his lordship appeared and conceal a fresh fall of cliff." It was just such a fall of cliff which contributed to Bute's death. While walking along their edge, part gave way and he dropped 28 feet, spraining his ankle. This took many months to heal and an illness during the following summer bade him return to London for medical advice. He died in London in March 1792 without returning to Highcliffe.

After lavishing a reputed £100,000 on Highcliffe for his own indulgence, he was to leave it to his fourth son, Charles, who would lack the resources to maintain such a leviathan on the income from a mere 100 acres and the salary of a soldier. While home on leave in 1778, Charles had married Louisa Bertie, daughter of Lord Vere Bertie. Their first son, also Charles, was born a year later and their second son, John, three years after that. His wife advised him to demolish those parts surplus to their means and sell the objects they did not need and in May 1793 the contents of the library were auctioned. However, his "thatched house" at nearby Bure Homage, town house in Whitehall and grace and favour residence in Richmond Park satisfied Charles' requirements. In 1794 he was promoted to Major-General with an important command in the Mediterranean and the subsequent capture of the Corsican fortress of Calvi, after which he was made Lieutenant-General in

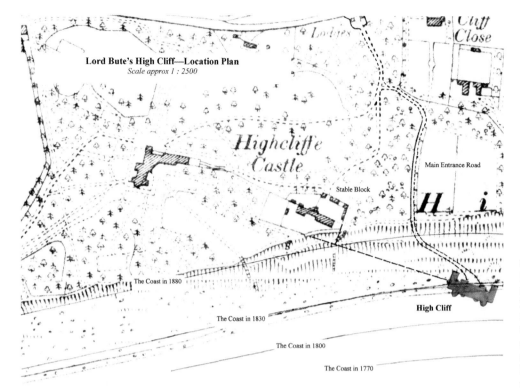

Lord Bute's High Cliff—Location Plan
Scale approx 1 : 2500

Supposition map by Frank Tyhurst, showing where the 3rd Earl's High Cliff would have been, the erosion of the cliffs since then, and the position of Lord Stuart's house, which replaced it.

Corsica. Highcliffe was sold in June 1795 to Gerard Levinge van Heythuysen, a lawyer from London, for reputedly a mere £12,000.

The purchaser set about selling the contents of both house and garden very peremptorily with an auction on site in August of the same year which lasted 11 days. Included in the sale were the garden buildings and long stretches of wall. Much of the walled garden survived, however, as did a porticoed temple. 8,000 individually named plants were offered for sale in pots and baskets as well as from the ground and these included trees in the shelter belt. One lot consisted of 240 firs, 100 planes, birches and other trees. The main areas of Bute's plantations were unaffected. The wood about 140 metres to the west of the house survived, as did the swathe of wooded parkland as far as the paired lodges on the Lymington road. Gilpin described the landscape in 1791:

> The road to the house runs directly to the front, narrow, and contracted at the entrance, but opening by degrees. The house first appears; then the lawn; which, though narrow in front, extends amply on both sides, with a pavilion at each extremity. These pavilions have a good effect from the sea, by giving consequence to the house. From the land they contribute, by marking the limits of the lawn, to open the idea more gradually. Beyond the lawn, the grand colonnade just mentioned [the Isle of Wight] extends; and beyond all, the expanse of the ocean. There is something very amusing in thus contemplating an idea, which is continually dilating and opening itself from a narrow tunnel into infinite space.

Previous pages: High Cliff from the north east, c. 1790. The conifers were planted as a windbreak to help protect Bute's collection of exotic plants.

94

Portrait of Charles
Stuart de Rothesay
after Johannes Pieter
de Frey.

Unfortunately he fails to mention the botanic collections which must have been
visible from the drive. He was too entranced with the picturesque nature of the special setting.

Van Heythuysen demolished both sets of most recent additions, reducing the
house to less than half of its previous volume. He died within two years and his widow later
sold the house to James Penleaze, a surgeon, who was able to afford it through a piece of
serendipity, a large sum of bank notes he found in a hat case. The house in its reduced state
survived into the first years of the nineteenth century. However, the remorseless approach
of the cliff-edge obliged Penleaze to build a new house about 200 metres to the north-west,
described by a future resident as "a very common-place rough cart-house". The site of Bute's
Highcliffe was overwhelmed by the sea.

General Charles Stuart was knighted for his services in the ongoing war in the
Mediterranean against Napoleon's forces and was consulted by Pitt on the future conduct
of the war. His plan to mount an offensive against Napoleon in Provence was accepted but

denied sufficient troops. He resigned his post in 1800 after objecting to plans to hand Malta back to the Russians. He died in 1801, "one of the great soldiers England has wasted".

His elder son, also Charles, was to have a successful diplomatic career which kept him abroad most of his life until 1830. The romantic notion that his undeviating ambition was to buy back the property owned by his grandfather and sold by his father may be overstated but the opportunity to start doing so from Penleaze came about from 1808. Although Penleaze had already sold on the lodges with a piece of land upon which a house called East Highcliffe had been built, this did not prevent Charles from eventually acquiring that land too in exchange for land at the other end of the estate. His mother was left to manage a sheep farm and brick-field while he, with the idea of filling a future grand home with worthy contents, collected furnishings and paintings, mainly from France where he was ambassador from 1815. His marriage in 1816 was to Lady Elizabeth Yorke, daughter of the 3rd Earl of Hardwicke, who had the background and accomplishments to fill the role of an ambassador's consort, and their two daughters were born in Paris: Charlotte in 1817 and Louisa in 1818. After returning from Paris he was appointed to the role of mediator between Portugal and Brazil to conclude a successful independence treaty between the two. Having been knighted some

The conservatory or winter garden facade of Lord Stuart's Highcliffe Castle, 2006.

96

A pair of gatehouses surviving from the 3rd Earl's High Cliff, 2006.

time before his marriage, he became Baron Stuart de Rothesay of the Isle of Bute under the premiership of the Duke of Wellington in the New Year of 1828. He was recalled to Paris as ambassador a few months later but, when Wellington resigned his premiership at the end of 1830, Stuart's post was terminated and he returned to England in 1831.

This gave him the opportunity of designing a new home to be known as Highcliffe Castle. With the architect, WJ Donthorn, and mostly in the absence of Lady Stuart who remained in their London home or with her ailing father, he devised a house inspired by stone sections and windows from three ancient structures in the Seine valley: the Gothic Abbey of Jumièges, the flamboyant renaissance manor of Les Andelys and the Medieval Church of St Vigor in Rouen. Their parts were selected and acquired by Lord Stuart and brought by barge across the Channel. Fanciful turrets, traceried balustrades and gargoyles decorated its roofline. It swallowed up the site of the house which Penleaze had constructed inland of the original Highcliffe and which the Stuarts were using when at the coast.

When viewed from the sea, a pair of towers on either side of a central elevated section were flanked by low wings, one of which ends in a substantial conservatory. The easterly tower was to be clumsily demolished in 1974 after the castle was ravaged by two fires in the late 1960s. The oriel window from Les Andelys is attached to the west tower above the main south porch and looks directly towards the vista of the Needles. The main body of the house backs onto a lofty structure reminiscent of the chapel of Eton College where Lord Stuart was educated, with buttresses, turrets and narrow ogee windows along its sides while a grand Medieval window was pierced in its northern end to diffuse light through stained glass brought from the Continent. It was designed as the imposing hallway to the north side of the house, entered under a colossal *porte-cochere*. When this castle was still inhabited as a private house in the 1940s, Christopher Hussey remarked: "As a setting for these gems Lord Stuart evolved a curious blend of perpendicular Gothic with Elizabethan. With its large windows and light skeleton, the building is curiously modern" and "sets livableness even before romantic character." The reaction of Lady Stuart was not as favourable as had been Lady Bute's to the previous house 50 years before. She bemoaned its lack of comfort and wished the whole thing had fallen over the cliff, but the work went on to be completed, doubtless with some deference to her wishes.

A network of drives radiated outwards from the porte-cochere. Towards the north-east departed the main drive, veering eastwards across parkland and swinging north up an avenue of Scots pine to leave through Bute's original lodges. This landscape survived until the 1950s. Due east ran a service drive to the stables and kitchen garden before connecting with the main drive. Westwards and then south-westwards a drive threaded the woods fronting the coast. One branch went to Steamer Lodge, the caprice of Lord Stuart who brought a redundant steamer to be wedged into a gap in the cliffs. The other turned north-west to leave

The grand entrance and *porte cochère* of Highcliffe Castle, inspired by Eton College chapel.

the estate at the junction of the main road and the lane to Mudeford and Bure Homage, the home of Stuart's youth. Due north ran a short straight avenue of holm oaks *Quercus ilex* to end in a perpendicular path and a screen of trees in front of the road. This truncated drive had probably been the main approach to Penleaze's new house.

Holm oaks were planted in profusion elsewhere on the estate by Lady Stuart who began to improve the grounds of Highcliffe by planting and making walks, sunken to shelter plants. Such paths still criss-cross the woods to the south-east of the castle. The choice of trees is likely to have been influenced and perhaps selected by Lord Stuart to remind him of his time as British Minister in Portugal in 1809. Even today the woods between the house and the cliff include many such specimens, some of considerable size where planted in the lee of other trees, and a fine avenue of holm oaks runs north from the lodges past St Mark's Church, itself a monument to Lord Stuart's munificence.

To the south-west, in the direction of the Needles, a vista was left open. As late as the 1940s one of the two porticoed temples inherited from the Bute landscape stood framed by the woodland at the western edge of this open space. Behind its eastern fringe of trees runs the north-west extension of the garden wall from the former Highcliffe, fronting kitchen gardens and stables which served both properties in interrupted succession and are now incorporated into the gardens of adjacent properties. Not only were the Stuarts de Rothesay supplied in London with vegetables sent by hamper from here, long before the arrival of the railways, but lemon trees and even potato tubers were introduced there by Lord Stuart through his contacts in Europe.

A formal terrace with fountain adjoined the house to the south overlooking a sunken garden with exotic plants in pots during the ownership of Louisa, the Stuarts' younger

Trees and shrubs protect the existing cliff below Highcliffe Castle from further erosion.

daughter. She was married to the 3rd Marquess of Waterford for 17 years until his death in a riding accident in 1859. She was left Highcliffe by her widowed mother in 1867, her elder sister, Viscountess Canning, having died in 1861 in India where her husband was Viceroy. To Louisa is credited the first serious stabilisation of the cliff-line. She ordered the construction of three or possibly four groynes, barriers to deflect the erosive effect of the rivers then flowing out of Christchurch Harbour as far as Highcliffe. Her greatest legacy was probably the establishment of the evergreen oak canopy on the cliff slopes themselves. By deflecting the rain water all year round and allowing an under-canopy to develop with which to bind the soil, this is the best tree for the purpose of stabilising the ground in this most hostile environment. In her choice of trees, she might have just been fortuitously following the example of her parents.

With no children from her or her sister's marriage, at her death in 1891 the inheritance was settled upon her second cousin, Edward Stuart Wortley, a descendent of the 3rd Earl

of Bute's second son, James, who would become Major-General during an active military career. To him is also credited significant sea defences to stabilise the cliff-line, involving very deep, shingle filled drains along the surface to take water away from the vulnerable cliff top, a system of open grips with slanting slides on the cliff slope itself and more groynes along the coast. As he reported to the Royal Commission on Coastal Erosion in 1908, he and his predecessor had spent £26,000 on various sea defence measures. During the occupation of both Louisa and Edward, celebrated visitors came to or stayed at Highcliffe. The Prince of Wales, the future Edward VII, came over from Osborne on the Isle of Wight, since Louisa was acquainted with the Royal Family through her sister's role as a lady-in-waiting to Queen Victoria. When Edward Stuart Wortley was away on military service and to supplement his income, Highcliffe was rented out for substantial periods. After a state visit to Britain in 1907, the German Emperor, Kaiser Wilhelm II, stayed at Highcliffe to recuperate from ill health on

Aerial view of Highcliffe Castle, c. 1950. Further housing has since covered much of the parkland in the middle right of the photograph.

100

the advice of his uncle, Edward VII, during which time he planted an oak in the estate, in the wake of other illustrious heads of state, King Alfonso XIII of Spain and Edward VII himself.

The cost of maintaining Highcliffe was already felt by Edward who began selling off land in the east of the estate for housing, built along roads with names associated with his family: Stuart, Waterford, Wharncliffe and Wortley. His widow, Violet, continued living at Highcliffe until the husband of her younger daughter, Bettine, the Earl of Abingdon, put the remainder of the estate on the market in 1950. Many of the contents were kept and eventually bequeathed to the Victoria and Albert Museum while the castle was converted to a children's convalescent home which proved unsuccessful. In 1953 it was sold again, with ten acres of surrounding land, to a Roman Catholic order, the Claretian Missionaries, to be used as a seminary. The remainder was sold for building land. The castle is now fringed on north and east by detached houses along a spine road called Rothesay Drive, following in stretches the original approach road from Bute's lodges. These, deprived of their *raison d'être*, now form part of a hotel and restaurant.

The Claretians initiated the removal of internal fittings by taking out the hall staircase to transform the room into the chapel it undoubtedly resembles and using part of it as steps in the path down the cliff. Following a fire in 1967, they moved out themselves because of insufficient recruits for the seminary. For sale again, the castle was purchased by three businessmen who applied unsuccessfully to demolish it and build 150 beach huts on the site and grounds. Another fire broke out, gutting the interior and leaving the structure open to the elements and further removal of its fittings. In 1977 Christchurch Borough Council purchased it for the value of its grounds which were soon opened to the public for the Queen's Silver Jubilee. The castle was left in its ruined state despite an offer by the Historic Buildings Council of a sizeable grant to help restore it. A repairs programme was at last begun in the 1990s with the support of English Heritage and the Heritage Lottery Fund. A heritage centre, substantially manned by volunteers, now educates the public about the fascination of Highcliffe's history and contents. Happily the one remaining artefact from the eighteenth century landscape, other than the walls of the kitchen garden, has recently been re-acquired by the Council and stands beyond the parterre when viewed from the house. It is the stone base of a sundial, for long placed at the edge of the cliff on the then supposed site of Lord Bute's mansion but sold in the 1960s. Carved with dolphins and ropes, its marine theme is a reminder of the third Earl's interest in nautical matters.

Its grounds, together with the woods west to Steamer Point, named after Lord Stuart de Rothesay's caprice, form a lynchpin of Christchurch Borough Council's coastal walk. The woods immediately surrounding the house have been largely retained although additions to the car park south of the house and the loss of trees in the storms of 1987 and 1990 have made gaps in the canopy. The approach to the castle now uses Penleaze's former avenue from the main road. The western walls of the kitchen garden separate the houses on Rothesay Drive from the castle grounds. A new wide zig-zag path from the edge of the vista down to the shoreline cuts a swathe through the cliff's protective vegetation but fulfils a dual role in helping to defend it with timber-fronted retaining walls while vestiges of the former Highcliffe staircase lie on the grass at its summit. Glancing eastwards, it is hard to believe that a substantial eighteenth century house and botanic garden ever existed just a short way along the coast.

Cardiff

The spire and towers of the castle form a fantasy Gothic backdrop to the southern end of Bute Park.

Cardiff owes its existence to the Butes. It has been said that no other city in Britain has been so influenced by one aristocratic family. Their association with the city began in the late eighteenth century through an adventitious marriage and subsequent entitlement to its castle and lands around the city. The coal which was extracted from mines on their enlarged and rationalised agricultural estates in the valleys north of Cardiff was exported from docks built by family money on family land. This investment fuelled enormous urban expansion in the nineteenth century. Their influence was not just limited to ownership. The Bute estate got involved in the development and design of large tracts of residential Cardiff including Cathedral Road, Pontcanna and Riverside on the other side of the River Taff from the castle and at Cathays to the east, which give the city a distinct style.

Previous pages: Behind the Norman keep and castle green is the twin towered north gate into Bute Park. The towers of Cathays Park, formerly owned by the Butes and now the city's civic centre, rise in the background. The remains of internal walls demolished in 1777 appear in the foreground.

Their most obvious landscape legacy is the open land they retained in the city centre. The castle grounds along the river north of the castle are now known as Bute Park. West across the river is Sophia Gardens, provided by the family as an amenity ground for the town's inhabitants, while the magnificent civic centre, Cathays Park, to the east of the castle, is built on former Bute park land sold to the city in the last decade of the nineteenth century. Cardiff's other great linear park at Roath was laid out on land mostly donated by the 3rd Marquess.

Cardiff developed at the lowest bridging point of the River Taff along the strategic route west into Wales on the relatively flat and fertile lands of the coastal plain. First descriptions of it are recorded by John Leland in his *Itinerary in Wales* of 1536–1539 and John Speed's map of the town of 1610 shows a little walled town scarcely wider than the castle enclosure and three times as long, bounded on the north by the castle. This has dominated and protected the town for nearly two millennia from when it was a Roman fort with a powerful stone wall, re-used and strengthened by the Normans who also built the motte and keep. It accommodated the Medieval shire hall within its walls, and the monastery of the Black Friars stood to its immediate west and that of the Grey Friars to the east. Its domestic premises date from the early fifteenth century when the Earl of Warwick built a new tower and hall block on the west of the castle enclosure. These were considerably improved and enlarged by the Herbert family, later Earls of Pembroke, in the late sixteenth century, when they were granted the castle and lands by Edward VI. The siding of the 4th Earl with the Parliamentary cause in the Civil War saved the castle from demolition, even though it had been occupied by the King towards the end of the war. Sadly, however, the Herberts lost interest in their Cardiff property as they concentrated their resources on Wilton House and their lands in southern Wiltshire. By the end of the eighteenth century the castle was in a dilapidated state.

In 1766 Viscount Mountstuart married Charlotte Windsor, daughter of Viscount Windsor and heir through her paternal grandmother to the Herbert lands in South Wales. In the 1770s he commissioned Lancelot 'Capability' Brown, the architect and landscape improver who had worked for his father at Luton and Highcliffe, to make improvements to his castle which he intended as the seat of residence of his eldest son, for whom he held political ambitions and who was indeed elected to the parliamentary seat of Cardiff in 1790. The thick stone wall connecting the Black Tower on the south of the ramparts to the keep in the north, which divided the castle enclosure in two, was blown up with gunpowder. The great building on the south of the keep, the remains of the shire hall and the accommodation for Medieval knights originally built by the Normans were also demolished.

The moat surrounding the motte was drained and filled in so that a simple green lawn remained on the floor of the enclosure, so bare and devoid of trees that, as one particularly acerbic traveller to Wales noted in 1787 "it seems to as only calculated for The Town Bowling Green". It was indeed sometimes used for that purpose. We know that by 1802 a shrubbery had been created and by 1815 plantings of trees also existed on the slopes leading up to the ramparts, on the slopes of the motte, and in the south of the green. A level gravel walk was laid along the ramparts to north and east beside the castellated walls which were low enough, however, to allow a view beyond. A spiral walk ascended to the keep.

Thomas White, described as an eminent plantsman, advised on the planting of the wider estate beyond the castle walls but expense prevented his plans being realised. A plan of 1790 shows a new approach road to the castle from the east and the turnpike road from the north being rerouted further east away from the castle. It was never implemented and may have been an alternative to a Brown plan for a grander approach to the castle. Brown's layout of the castle green that did get implemented was the carriage way approach from the south gate, completed 1789, and its exit by a tunnel constructed through the wall to the north of the motte in the early nineteenth century.

It seems that Mountstuart intended the 'improved' castle grounds to be enjoyed by the public from the start. One visitor in 1794 remarked that the grounds had been laid out in walks "for the convenience of the inhabitants of this place" and a guide book of 1802 described

View from The Mount in 1828 with the residential quarters on the left, after Henry Holland's alterations.

the walks as being kept in clean order, "and afford to the inhabitants of Cardiff an excellent promenade exhibiting a beautiful and diversified view in every direction... the walks are open and at all hours free to anyone." Although never realised, the keep's metamorphosis into a ballroom with a copper roof had been considered for "the gratification of the gentry... as a more commodious assembly room than that in the town hall". In his concern for the inhabitants, Mountstuart, who was created the 1st Marquess in 1796, was carrying out his duties as Lord of the Castle, a role which, until the Municipal Reform Act of 1835, conferred on him and his successor the right, directly or indirectly, to appoint all the officers of the borough.

From 1783 Henry Holland continued the works of modernising and refining the castle after the death of Brown, his father-in-law. He re-built the north wing of the residential quarters, added a corresponding wing to the south and divided the Medieval Great Hall into an entrance hall, a library and dining room. The refurbished residence was, however, never inhabited by the family since Mountstuart preferred to stay in local inns, The Cardiff Arms or The Angel, both owned by him. When his heir was killed in 1794, the death so affected him that he proceeded to neglect his estate in south Wales, only appearing to do his duty to the county to which he had been appointed Lord Lieutenant in 1797 when a French force landed at Fishguard in west Wales. For the training of the militia, he allowed the castle to be used as a parade ground.

His agents acquired strategic land in various parts of Cardiff on his behalf, including the site of the Grey Friars and of Cathays Park, just to the east of the castle. With his second wife, Fanny Coutts, he stayed in the rebuilt Cathays House at the north end of the park, approached by a fine avenue from the south. No plans for it survive, however, and his grandson, the 2nd Marquess, demolished it in 1824 before it was ever fully completed. The park was then surrounded by a wall and its internal hedges removed so as to create open parkland except on the north-east where Dobbins Pit was retained as a farm. A kitchen garden was also laid out near The Friars for fruit and vegetables for the family's households both in Cardiff and their other properties throughout the nineteenth century. Fruit trees were also planted beside the kitchen garden.

Cathays Park, historically separated from the castle and grounds by the Merthyr road entering Cardiff from the north and, from 1794, by the Glamorganshire Canal, was long to be coveted by borough councillors as the location for a public park but its shrewd retention by the Butes until the 1890s ensured that a rare and precious opportunity would arise for the development of a civic centre set within a fine landscape in the twentieth century.

Unlike his grandfather, the 2nd Marquess dedicated himself to the management of his enormous properties in south Wales and is given the accolade of founder of modern Cardiff. During his first journey to the town in 1815 after inheriting the title, he commissioned a survey of his lands by David Stewart who recommended him to rationalise his scattered land holdings and build up a single estate. Stewart also emphasised that enormous potential mineral

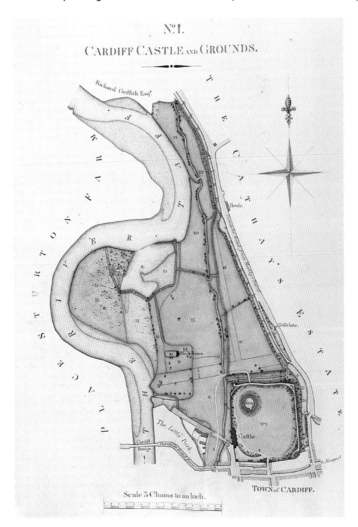

Cardiff Castle and Grounds from David Stewart's Report, 1824. Within a few years of this plan, the river had been straightened. A loss of land to the castle grounds in the convex curve of the river was compensated by a substantial gain of land at its concave curve further north.

wealth lay under much of the Marquess' property further up the river valleys at the same time that he owned most of the land surrounding the Taff estuary. Their joint exploitation would work to his advantage.

The Glamorganshire canal, financed by the iron masters of Merthyr Tydfil, had been completed to Cardiff for the shipment of their finished iron products, replacing expensive pack-horse transport. It was extended four years later into a basin for sea-going ships since the river quays often silted up. This was the pre-cursor of the docks. The profits made on the lease of his coalfields in the western tributary valleys of the Taff convinced the Marquess of the potential earnings from a coal-handling dock suitable for larger vessels. Before the end of 1834, a dock feeder canal passing close to the castle was cut to bring water from the Taff and flush out any sediment which would accumulate in the West Dock he was financing.

The 3rd Marquess as a young boy in front of Cardiff Castle.

The dock opened in 1839 but was so over-budget that the Marquess was obliged to mortgage part of his Glamorgan estates. Faults in its construction delayed its full operation until 1843. By dint of land-ownership he was able to coerce most of the coal freight then using the recently opened Taff Valley Railway to supply his dock, with such effect that by 1849 the ships had to queue to find a berth. Despite this ultimate material success, aged only 54 the Marquess died of a heart attack attributed to the stress of his financial risks.

Stewart, the surveyor, had also suggested retaining Cooper's Field, north of the castle, as open land sufficient for a nobleman's seat. Although this land had for centuries accommodated mills, rope-walks, and a tannery, it had always been prone to serious flooding and had to remain as open pasture. Only nine of the 43 acres of castle grounds at that time were above the level of floods and these he recommended should be constantly kept in grass, being under the castle walls. The mill stream ran along the east of the flood plain under the elevated bank, passing the west walls of the castle and flowing under the west gate into the town. A new bridge in 1795–1796 across the river had not solved all the danger of flooding so that the Justices of the Peace kept recommending that a new cut be made to divert the water straight through the old course of the river. Stewart suggested that the banks along the course of the river be raised to prevent overflowing.

By the time of the 1829 plan, which showed that the mill stream was to be adapted as the dock feeder canal, the double bend in the river had been straightened. Seven years later Blackweir Farm, a further extension of the castle grounds northwards, was acquired by the Marquess, probably to secure the course of the upper reaches of the dock feeder which

The Clock Tower,
Cardiff Castle.

was fed by the river at a point at the northern edge of the farm. By 1851 the river was following the course which it does today and drainage works were in progress in those parts of the grounds which had been occupied by the former bed of the stream.

The building of the new bridge was followed by the destruction of some cottages close to the castle to improve the views westwards. The removal of other buildings constructed against and in the castle walls, even within the moat, was a continuous project undertaken by the 1st and 2nd Marquesses to allow the castle to stand clear of the huddle of houses. It was the 3rd Marquess who reaped the rewards and could pursue his plans for the reconstruction of the walls and moat.

In 1865, the year that John Patrick, 3rd Marquess, went up to Oxford, he met the architect William Burges. Already internationally renowned for his designs of St Finbar's

Cathedral in Cork, Burges was zealous in promoting a version of Gothic architecture based on that of Medieval France. He was asked for suggestions to improve the southern wall of the castle and reported to the Trustees of the Estate in 1866. The option chosen was to conserve what existed but to make additions consistent with its use "as a nobleman's residence". Remaining cottages were removed and the walls were carefully restored and finished with battlements. A tall clock tower was erected "which would form a handsome object at the present entrance to the town and cut up the long line of the unbroken wall". The use of dark Caerphilly stone for most of the reconstructions or extensions made the new build distinct from the original fabric.

The main facade of the castle, c. 1890. Its walls are smothered in vines. In front of the moat is the Animal Wall, which has since been re-built beyond the Clock Tower in the distance.

This honest practice, pursued by John Patrick in most of his re-creations, was in line with the principles of William Morris and enshrined in the recommendations of the Society of Ancient Buildings he was to found with Philip Webb in 1877. The partial reconstruction of the layout of the Greyfriars Monastery, which he carried out within the grounds, identified the base of the walls in brick rather than stone.

The site of the moat was partially excavated and Burges recommended a Medieval flower garden with raised beds enclosed within walls of stone. Some would have flowers, others only grass, while a few would have grass with holes for the insertion of flower pots. A long bed was to run at the foot of the wall with a trellis for creeping plants and espaliers. A fountain and statue in the highest raised bed were mentioned. All were to be separated from the road by iron railings and strong handsome piers. These details remained a fantasy. In practice grape vines were trained far up the walls which rise from the moat and a wall was built on the west side of the castle entrance in front of the moat garden. Designed by Burges in 1866, it was refined and executed after his death in 1882 by William Frame and carved by Thomas Nicholls, its stone animals engagingly peering over alternate merlons along its battlemented crest. To allow for the widening of the street in 1922–1923, the Animal Wall was then relocated further west to enclose the south side of the grounds between the bridge and the castle and extended by the addition of six extra animals. This parade of birds and beasts continue to delight pedestrians with their elegant pose and concentrated gaze on both sides of the castellated West Gate, an entrance to the park straight off the street, erected in 1860 to the designs of Alexander Roos, architect to the Bute estate at that time.

A stone panther poised to leap over the Animal Wall.

Bird's-eye view of the gothicised stables north of the castle by Axel Haig, c. 1870. They are now occupied by the Welsh College of Music and Drama. In the foreground is a glimpse of the dock feeder canal while behind a boat sails along the Glamorgan Canal, now emptied and used at this point as a car park. Cathays Park behind is still shown as open fields.

After the marriage of his patron in 1872, Burges' designs for the rest of the castle began to be implemented, strongly tempered by the recommendations of Bute himself who wanted extra rooms to be in towers. New ones, therefore, needed to be built and the existing Herbert, Octagon and Bute towers were heightened, creating the irregular, romantic roofline of today. On top of the Bute Tower an exotic roof garden was laid out, inspired, according to his biographer and friend, the Rev. Hunter Blair, by the roof garden of a Maronite bishop in the Levant, visited by the 3rd Marquess in 1866. It is floored with mosaics and a band of pink marble marks the step down into the sunken centre. Polychrome tiles cover the walls under the surrounding covered walkway and describe events from the life of Elijah with inscriptions in Hebrew, a language which John Patrick was learning at the time. In the centre is Burges' multi-tiered bronze fountain, cast in 1876 and featuring four beavers clutching fish and expelling streams of water from their mouths, a fond reference to Mount Stuart and its wildlife.

Within the castle walls the keep was repaired in 1872–1873 and the moat re-excavated. A flight of stone steps were constructed against the motte to allow easier access to the keep. Influenced by the fourteenth century wooden bridge at Lucerne, Burges also designed the Swiss Bridge, built between 1875–1878, to connect the domestic apartments in the west of the castle to the garden across the moat without fundamentally altering the historic fabric of the house. It complimented in appearance the wooden gallery which had been designed to run along the south wall of the castle. The reconstruction of the West Gate by the 4th Marquess in 1921 encroached on the setting of the bridge under the west wall of the castle. In 1927 the bridge was removed to a site across the dock feeder canal between the castle and the stables but was demolished in 1963 after being vandalised, despite much misgiving but in the interests of safety and cost-cutting by an insensitive council.

By 1855 the Trustees of the Estate had acquired all the land north of the castle and between the river and the Glamorgan canal as far as Gabalfa and Llandaff, a tongue of land some two miles in length. During that decade the Trustees started to restrict access which the public had previously enjoyed to the castle grounds. As Cardiff's population grew and the incidence of abuse to the gardens increased, the castle green was eventually closed to give the family greater privacy, as was the land north of the castle including Cooper's Field. This was described by someone born in 1844 as, "stretching away in one green expanse as far as the eye could reach in the direction of Llandaff. No hedges or other artificial meadow, with the exception of the Feeder, intersected this virgin meadow, and in summer particularly, it was the recognised place for a stroll".

Partly as compensation for the withdrawal of public access, 24 acres of land on the west bank of the river was laid out as a public walk to designs by Alexander Roos. They were named Sophia Gardens in honour of the widow of the 2nd Marquess and the estate paid for their lay out and maintenance. An avenue of limes ran the entire length of the grounds to join a narrower path around a lake formed from part of the old double bend of the river. Opened in 1857, they were hailed as the first public pleasure grounds in Wales. A trustee attributed their idea to the 10 year old John Patrick: "Some few years ago he passed a season on the Continent with his mother and there he saw the large parks which are devoted to the public. On his return to England his desire was that a public park should be added to Cardiff." On her only visit Lady Bute gave instructions for a fountain to be erected in the centre. A portion of the gardens was

A fine avenue of limes planted by Pettigrew along the path leading from the southern entrance to Bute Park.

laid out as a bowling green, one of the first projects to be undertaken by Andrew Pettigrew who arrived from Dumfries House to take charge of the castle grounds in 1873. Six years later the park was extended northwards for sporting use into what was called Sophia Gardens Field.

Between 1851 and 1870 part of Cooper's Field was developed as a deer park. The animals succeeded in escaping at least once despite the high metal fencing which enclosed them. Some tree planting had already taken place but Old Man's wood, to the west, evolved

through natural regeneration and the main formal planting is alongside the track to the north of the castle. By 1881 three distinct tree roundels had been planted in the north of Cooper's Field, perhaps inspired by those at Dumfries House. Two have since been incorporated into larger planted areas with the southern one, a group of Turkey oaks, *Quercus cerris*, still distinguishable.

After Pettigrew's arrival the reputation of the grounds was enhanced by garden journals which ran articles describing his influence. He was a regular contributor to their pages himself. The overall design of the landscape was based on stretches of uninterrupted lawn,

Coopers Field in Bute Park looking north, an example of Pettigrew's massed planting of trees bordering expanses of grass along which views were directed up towards the distant hills.

either punctuated with irregular shaped clumps of ornamental trees or flowing between more substantial stands of trees along which views were directed towards the castle's Gothic towers or up the Taff towards the hills. The circuit of pathways encouraged appreciation of the specimen plant collection and presented a variety of vistas. Pettigrew's accomplishments are all the more impressive when account is taken of the marshy state of much of the land on his arrival in Cardiff. The *Gardener's Magazine* explained in 1899 that to fill in the hollows and depressions and bring them to a height well above water level had been a task of considerable magnitude. It required the carting of many thousands of loads of soil into the grounds from various building sites throughout the fast developing town. By 1901, two years before Pettigrew's death, the framework of today's tree planting had been established under his direction. The network of driveways was finalised with the excavation of the Friary site and the formal avenues of lime-trees planted alongside.

A visitor to the castle keep can look north from its summit towards the cleft in the hills formed by the Taff Gorge and just pick out the towers of Castell Coch like an eye-catcher within the wider landscape of the former Bute domain. Of thirteenth century origins, it was surveyed in 1850 by GT Clark the pioneer of British castle studies. His report provided the basis for the excavations commissioned by John Patrick 20 years later and the plans produced by Burges in 1872 to restore the ruins and make an extravagant folly for the Butes' occasional occupation in the summer. Work started in 1875. French influence shows in its pepper pot towers with steep conical roofs and in some of its interiors. The idea of elevated external timber walkways within the courtyard was, however, borrowed from his drawings of Medieval castles of central Europe observed during his earlier travels and also used in the Swiss Bridge and along Cardiff Castle ramparts.

Although the structure was largely complete by 1879, the fitting out of the interiors was just beginning when Burges died. It was carried on by a team of craftsmen who had previously worked for Burges. William Frame, his pupil, who later worked at House of Falkland, remained to oversee the work. Historic subjects in the statues and paintings are important but animals and flowers proliferate. There are charming panels of individual flowers in the wainscoting of the drawing room while above them are exuberant representations of plants, up to the lower cornice of this lofty, vaulted space, acting as a setting for depictions of Aesop's fables. The aquamarine ceiling is a sky against which birds glide, compartmentalised by stone ribs up which progress lines of butterflies. The domed ceiling of Lady Bute's bedroom is rich in panels of fruit-laden branches with symbolic significance. The second row of panels depicts vines billowing with bunches of black grapes, a reference to the viticultural activities of Medieval castles in general and Castell Coch in particular.

One of Andrew Pettigrew's first tasks after his appointment at Cardiff was to visit the Bordeaux region of France to study wine-growing. For antiquarian reasons and, perhaps, inspired by his father-in-law's memories of the vineyard of the Dukes of Norfolk, John Patrick determined to experiment with growing grapes. The first vines were planted up the walls of Cardiff Castle and by 1875 were already loaded with grapes for wine production. The vineyard on steeply sloping land below Castell Coch was planted that year and by 1877 was also productive. Pettigrew described the long rows of vines with "the tops of the canes all

Vineyard below
Castell Coch,
c. 1900.

neatly stopped at the height of four feet from the ground with their dark glossy foliage almost
meeting in the rows" and were "a sight not to be seen anywhere else in the county."

Excited by this initial success, Bute instructed his gardener to plant further vineyards
in other parts of his estate, but only at Swanbridge was there progress. Years followed when
the wood hardly ripened and disease became a problem. Punch satirised this experiment:

> The Marquess of Bute has, it appears, a Bute-iful vineyard at Castell Coch
> near Cardiff where it is to be hoped that in future Hock will be superseded
> by Coch and the un-pronounceable vintages of the Rhine will yield to
> the un-pronounceable vintages of the Taff. Cocheimer is as yet a wine
> in potential but the vines are planted and the gardener, Mr. Pettigrew,
> anticipates no petty growth.

A great pleasure for the family was to provide their guests with the unusual past-
time of participating in the grape harvest. Hunter Blair reported that "We spent a whole
afternoon in the pressing house picking to pieces bunches of choice grapes which were to be
made into wine for the use of the altar...." In 1920, the vines were eventually removed.

John Patrick enjoyed taking strenuous walks at all his properties. It was not unusual
for him to walk over five miles from Cardiff Castle to Castell Coch and back along roughly
the route close to the east bank of the river taken by the present-day Taff Trail, a dedicated
track for cyclists and pedestrians. When he died, Castell Coch was where his widow and
daughter resided until succession to the family estates was settled. From then on it was only

The drawbridge
entrance to Castell
Coch, 2007.

occasionally occupied during the summer. Later in the year it was used as a meeting point for the Pentyrch Hunt, of which the 4th Marquess was a long-standing patron and his wife its Master in the 1930s. Beech woods still clothe the land immediately surrounding the castle, just as they did when first photographed in 1870.

The marriage to Charlotte Windsor by the 1st Marquess in the late eighteenth century had also procured Caerphilly Castle for the family, situated in the Rhymney Valley only four miles north of Castell Coch across a neck of hills. This had been one of the truly great thirteenth century strongholds of Europe, later abandoned. Deterioration through war damage and stone removal through the centuries was compounded by slumping of parts of the structure when its defensive lakes dried out following the neglect of the sluice-gates. The great hall was re-roofed and all the ruins fully recorded by John Patrick but it was his son who undertook its restoration between 1928 and 1937, rebuilding large sections in a composite stone to distinguish new build from old. Landscaping formed part of the programme with the demolition of properties against the castle wall as their leases expired and plans for the re-flooding of the lakes. This was ultimately completed in the late 1960s when the State assumed responsibility for its care and the great hall was restored.

The 4th Marquess also showed his interest in architecture and archaeology at Cardiff Castle where in 1917 he excavated the old mill leat to the west of the castle and had earlier reconstructed the North Gates from the castle green into the park. At the north of Cooper's Field a new walled garden was laid out between 1906 and 1917. Its unfortunate location continues to break the flow of the landscape even today, despite having provided a useful depot for the city's Parks Department and now an education centre for visitors a horticultural training centre for staff. South of it was planted up an orchard to replace those lost in the Cathays Park sale of 1897. The family's hothouses on the Greyfriars site had remained in use until 1905, however, since that land had not been included in the sale.

Although the orchard is no more, adjacent to the walled garden are collections of crataegus, flowering cherries, malus and sorbus which bear it witness with their blossoms and bright berries. These smaller species are complimented by a collection of oak, ash, beech, hornbeam and acer to west and east of the park, and pines beside the stand of mature pines in the middle southern part. They comprise the Arboretum, developed by William Nelmes, Director of Parks, since the city acquired the park after the Second World War. The Tree Register of Great Britain has described the park as one of the most interesting and varied in the country in which there are 37 champion trees from the first phase of post-war planting.

By the 1920s, the Blackweir Farm lands were levelled and converted to playing fields, a gesture towards the occasional re-use, by invitation, of the grounds by the public. The tall belt of trees, including some impressive evergreen oaks, which has surrounded this open space to north and west since the late nineteenth century, screens the views across the river to Pontcanna Fields. These 'fields' are also used for team sports and informal recreation and across them stride avenues of lime and horse-chestnut in the direction of Llandaff Cathedral. To the south of Pontcanna Fields, the original layout of Sophia Gardens has been adapted to the demands of national sports buildings and accompanying hard car-parking to service them. To the east of the castle extends Cathays Park, now the elegant collection of public buildings in Portland stone aligned along two wide avenues with, at its core, a rectangular park centred on an elaborate war memorial, the Temple of Peace and Health.

Roath Park in north-east Cardiff, similarly aligned along a north-south valley, was also developed with the assistance of the Butes. In a case of enlightened self-interest, a group of landowners donated this stretch of boggy land surrounded by fields to the city, foremost among them being the 3rd Marquess. His purchase of 80 acres from the Trustees of his estate and presentation to the public formed the bulk of the park's 130 acres. His wife cut the first sod in 1887 and the park was formally opened by their eldest son on his 13th birthday in 1894. On both sides of the linear park could then be developed comfortable middle class homes with attractive views onto water and trees. In line with Bute Park, Roath Park today contains many interesting tree and plant species. A further tribute to the family in Cardiff is the lovely pelargonium of very dark purple, velvety petals rimmed with rose, bred in the city by W Arthur Treseder in 1911 and called "Lord Bute". Less celebrated are the cultivars "Marchioness of Bute", similar with frilly edges, and the "Marquess of Bute", a variegated form of Lord Bute.

The Butes severed their links with Cardiff and South Wales over several years. After attempts by the 4th Marquess to offload the docks to the Corporation as early as 1906, they were eventually amalgamated with the railways under the Great Western railway company. In 1938 they received compensation for the nationalisation of the mineral reserves under the land they owned in South Wales and in the same year most of the urban estate in Cardiff was sold. The Black Tower of the castle was requisitioned by the army during the war and the grounds were converted by the estate to growing crops as part of the war effort, while the whole set of buildings escaped almost unscathed the intense bombing of the docks. Two years after the war ended, the 4th Marquess died. One of the first acts of the 5th Marquess was to present Cardiff Castle to the "Lord Mayor, Aldermen and citizens of Cardiff" in September of the same year.

Despite not being deliberately intended from the start as a positive piece of urban planning, the land-holding practices of the Butes resulted in a series of distinct pieces of land in the city centre being available for the construction of a civic centre on a green field site, space for intensive and extensive sporting facilities and a linear river park culminating in a fairy-tale castle. In 1924 unsuccessful plans to drive a new road through the Castle grounds and provide a new river crossing were challenged by the representative of the Bute estates using these emotive terms: "It is not like crossing a meadow. It is crossing a miniature Hampton Court—a really beautiful garden."

As part of a project of restoring the grounds of the castle to how they were under the Butes, it is intended to re-open the North Gates of the castle so that the public can move directly between the castle and the park. Water from the mill leat that once flowed into the moat under the great west walls but was drained in the 1970s for reasons of flooding beyond the castle is to fill it again, reinstating the romantic reflections and illusions of a Medieval castle. Alexander Roos's castellated West Gate has undergone repairs and extensions to serve the needs of visitors since this has become the main pedestrian entrance into the park. The enchanting Animal Wall has been cleaned and the long nose of the anteater repaired. Work to reinstate the 3rd Marquess' partial ground level restoration of the Blackfriars Monastery is to be put in hand and recognition of the importance of the Arboretum is leading to better signage of the trees. With the assistance of a significant grant from the Heritage Lottery Fund, the Cardiff Council today is ensuring that the legacy of the Butes is being cherished.

Lord Bute
pelargonium.

Falkland

This estate of 1900 hectares, in the Kingdom of Fife, is an unusual mix of the palace—a royal hunting lodge—its park, and a mid-nineteenth century house surrounded by a formal garden within a picturesque landscape. The Royal Burgh of Falkland, with its small stone houses, lies between the palace and the house on the south side of the Maspie Burn, but on the north side there is a charming walkway alongside its bank which links the two. From the house, to the south and west, the Lomond Hills rise steeply, part-clad with trees, now part of the Lomond Hills Regional Park, while to the north the wide flat valley, the site of the Medieval hunting wood, is productive farm land.

Panorama from east Lomond looking over the town and House of Falkland early twenty-first century.

The palace had become the property of James I of Scotland in 1425, and was for many of the Stuart kings a favourite place from where to ride out hawking and chasing the deer. Looking out from the battlements to the north, it is still possible to imagine the park with its great oaks stretching out over the plains to the River Eden. In the fifteenth century the practice had been to release roebuck and stags carried in litters from other royal parks along with wild boar especially brought from France. During the following century, under the regency of Mary of Guise, there was a programme of renewal of the oak forest, so that by the seventeenth century it was one of the most important of their parks, stocked with fallow and red deer, with boars and swans. On the hill to the west of House of Falkland are a number of parallel earthworks called The Trenches into which deer may have been herded from the hills to be released for the hunt. Sir David Lindsay had written verse in 1530 as a celebration:

Previous pages: Looking north east from the Lomond Hills over the palace and town of Falkland. The deer park is beyond with its high deer-proof paling extending to the right of the castle. Alexander Keirincx 1640.

> Fare weill Faulkland, the forteress of Fyfe,
> Thy polite park under the Lowmound law,
> Sum tyme in thee I led ane lustie lyfe,
> The fallow deir to see them raike in row.

Charles I commissioned a new garden at the palace in 1628 with sundials and pillars and, though the last monarch to have stayed there was Charles II, crowned king of the Scots in 1651, the palace is still owned by the sovereign. With scant regard for the landscape, Cromwell's soldiers cut down the oaks in the park to build a fort at Perth and from 1652 the land ceased to be used for hunting. In the absence of the monarch the palace has been looked after by hereditary keepers, one of whom, Sir David Murray, built the original house of Nuthill to the west of the town in 1612, eventually replaced by the House of Falkland.

Though the two estates were always closely linked, they only became united under one owner in 1820. Professor John Bruce bought the right to be hereditary keeper of Falkland Palace and the following year acquired Nuthill Estate. Gradually throughout the nineteenth century more land was purchased, a new house was built, and finally the estate was sold to the 3rd Marquess of Bute in 1887, who was particularly interested in renovating the palace. The present hereditary keeper is Ninian Crichton Stuart, a great grandson of the 3rd Marquess, who is also steward of the whole Falkland Estate.

Bruce, who came from Fife, had made his fortune through the East India Company. He was an MP in Cornwall as well as fellow of the Royal Societies in London and Edinburgh. Although he lived in London, he maintained a house in the New Town, Edinburgh, where his niece and heir Margaret lived. She had been born in India, daughter of his brother Robert, through a liaison with a local lady. On acquiring the keepership of the palace Bruce began to restore the crumbling building, incurring the disapproval of his former pupil, Sir Walter Scott, for interfering with its romantic appearance. In order to protect the stone fabric from being plundered he built an eight foot high wall around the palace with two gates. In doing so the palace was now separated from its park, where sheep rather than deer now grazed. He also laid out a productive kitchen and flower garden in the grounds and established a tree nursery.

The old house at Nuthill was described in 1821 as a "beautiful place with a garden in the best order and many very fine trees". Even so, John Swinton, Bruce's builder, improved its setting by including a new north entrance drive and stables around a courtyard with accommodation to house the factor. The lime avenue at the east entrance near the town was probably planted then, and the burn next to the house was "dressed up in a very beautiful manner indeed by straightening its course and forming little cascades".

General improvements took place throughout the estate over the following 30 years as more land was acquired. In the six years leading up to his death in 1826 Bruce developed the picturesque nature of the landscape and made it more accessible. Three burns run down through rocky outcrops from the Lomond Hills through the grounds, the largest being the Maspie. He began by straightening part of this water course, building wooden bridges over it, planting its banks, laying out walks, and possibly at this time creating the "sublime" tunnel, with its kink. This walk led up the ravine to the Yad waterfall, a spectacular feature crowning the upper Maspie Den. Here a long thin gush of water emerges from the middle of a semi-circular rock set into the landscape, undercut to form a cave with a path around its interior.

Margaret Bruce, who was skilled at management, continued developing the landscape after her uncle's death and her subsequent marriage to Onesiphorus Tyndall, a barrister, in 1828. Onesiphorus, the second son of a Bristol banker, was an intimate friend of the 2nd Marquess

Yad waterfall. Early
twentieth century.

of Bute, a fellow Etonian with whom he toured Russia in 1813. So close was their friendship that
with Tyndall alone did he authorise his Cardiff estate officials to discuss his affairs, and in his
will appointed him as one of his trustees. Though the Tyndall Bruces never lived full time in
Falkland, with other homes in Edinburgh and Bristol and a passion for travel, they nevertheless
took an active role in estate development, planting over 1.5 million trees. These were brought
on in nursery grounds at the palace and elsewhere on the estate.

Fruit and vegetables were being grown in the hothouses, built in 1830 within the
palace grounds, and the gardener Alex Temple would regularly send boxes to the Tyndall
Bruces wherever they were staying. These included pineapples, apricots and melons. An
ornamental flower garden was planted in the palace courtyard. The whole estate had achieved
such advances in agriculture by 1845 that they were noted in the Statistical Account as being
the most significant for any parish in the county of Fife. It cannot have been a coincidence
that the Tyndall Bruces' friend, the 2nd Marquess, was also making similar advances in forestry
and farming at the same time on his estates.

Soon after their marriage Margaret and Onesiphorus decided that Nuthill should
be replaced by a new house. They took considerable time before settling on an architect and
design which they liked, as they dithered about whether to restore the palace as their residence
instead. In 1839 William Burn, a Scottish architect with successful commissions throughout
Britain including work at Mount Stuart for the 2nd Marquess, submitted detailed plans for a
new house. Work started almost immediately. Stone was mostly sourced from local quarries.
Painters and glaziers and other tradesmen from Edinburgh completed the interiors. The house
is a masterpiece of the 'Jacobethan' style, Burn's speciality, and reflected a trend within British
buildings to borrow Elizabethan and Jacobean styles, at a time when both architecture and
garden design, closely linked together, were undergoing an historical revival. William Sawrey

House of Falkland,
east parterre showing
the dressed ground
beyond. Early
twentieth century.

Gilpin, landscape designer and author, visited Burn at Falkland in September 1840 and gave some advice, probably with respect to the siting of the house and its view-points to the Lomond Hills, but it was another who would be credited with the actual garden layout.

Alexander Roos was commissioned to design the garden and landscape in an Italianate style with an emphasis on formality in the parterre next to the house. Burn objected to Roos' first design but soon accepted an alternative, indicating the importance he put on the immediate setting of the house. The choice of plants was left to an expert, Donald Beaton, another Scot, who was then the head gardener at Shrubland Park in Suffolk, where he had created spectacular flower beds. He was particularly renowned for his skill in bedding plants and his expertise in hybridisation had even come to the attention of Charles Darwin, who described him as a "clever fellow and damned cocksure man".

Roos wanted to use a variety of shells, coloured marbles, quartz, glass and granite as well as brick dust, coal and copper ores in the parterre design, in the spirit of Elizabethan gardens. Yet it is not clear how many of these materials were used. When the garden was illustrated soon after its completion in *The Book of the Garden* in 1853, the description only mentions the planting of scarlet geraniums, verbenas and showy plants, two ends laid out in sand and gravel paths. There are also minor differences between the published and actual layout, but the pyramidal yews, which survive today, are part of the Roos planting.

The author Charles M'intosh described the garden as "the most perfect specimen of a flower garden in Scotland, although on a small scale". It had three parterres with square piers on which there were vases, and was surrounded in part by a wall with stone urns. On the east and west parterres Roos designed two different large circular Italianate stone fountains, sculpted by John Howie of Edinburgh. Water spouting from a lion's mouth into a scallop shell and spilling over into another basin on the lower level of the west side completed the range of fountains. All were fed from a small reservoir on the hill above the south side of the house. This provided a great deal of pressure to the water works, as well as ample supplies for the house and for emergencies in case of fire. With input from the Tyndall Bruces, Roos laid out the rising dressed ground beyond to the south in a natural style starting with a carpet of grass, and leading on to rhododendrons and other flowering and evergreen shrubs, finally tapering up into the woods. The further development of the picturesque landscape up into the glen, with its paths, little bridges and seats, may also be attributed to him.

He also had a hand in the interior decoration of the house and later designed, in 1849, the Temple of Decision above the house to the west. This small stone garden building, since collapsed, which had a wide vista over the house, town, palace, and countryside, was set into the side of Greenhill. It was approached across a pasture and seen framed by trees. It had

The Temple of Decision. Late nineteenth century.

a Grecian pediment and slate roof with ornamental peak ridging tiles, and inside there were stone flags on the floor. Ninian Crichton Stuart suggests that the significance of the temple relates to Margaret's birth in India, where temples are usually sited at high points for their physical perspective to inspire the spirit to make good decisions.

On the death of Onesiphorus in 1855 a monument was placed on the adjacent Blackhill, with sight lines between the two eye-catchers and from the valley below. In 1858 Margaret Tyndall Bruce bought the last significant piece of land with orchard to complete the estate, Balmblae. It lies to the north of the Maspie Burn as it flows through the town, and connected House of Falkland with the palace.

As a boy, John Patrick, the 3rd Marquess, had visited Falkland with his mother in the 1850s, and later with Lady Elizabeth Moore, his guardian. Fascinated by its history he had written a paper on David, Duke of Rothesay, the hapless heir of Robert III who had been starved to death in the palace in 1402. He was well versed in the romantic history of its buildings and landscape. However, in 1888, after buying the estate, he noted that he was surprised that his recollections were not more vivid since it seemed larger, finer and the palace more imposing than he remembered. John Patrick considered House of Falkland his most "luxurious" of homes. It had mature gardens and parkland with a considerable number of exotic species: a tulip tree, a sequoia, and a Douglas fir of 59 feet in height, possibly the tallest in Britain. His prime reason for its purchase was the pleasure of restoring the palace, a Stuart property, but he also was considering the interests of his younger son Ninian for whom he wanted to provide an estate.

Bute was very disappointed by the work already done on the palace. To make a better and more complete restoration he engaged John Kinross, an architect, who subsequently worked on a number of his other projects. This involved major archaeological excavations, which revealed the cellars of the east wing and most of the palace foundations. Considerable scholarship preceded all of John Patrick's renovations of ruined sites so that new building work could be carried out without interfering with the historic fabric. At Falkland this included stripping all the ivy off the ancient palace walls to the disapproval of visitors, who seemed to prefer its 'ruined picturesque' look.

When he died in 1900 the restoration was partly completed with a new courtyard facade to the east range, a newly restored Cross House, and the careful rebuilding of the royal tennis court, the oldest in the world. Visitors paid to view the palace and the fees were donated to the University of St Andrews. In the palace garden a circle of oak trees were planted on the north end of the top lawn, which may represent the original Queens Quarrels, a clump, which was know to have been here. Quarrels are the arrows used in crossbows. A pergola was constructed as part of an ornamental fruit and flower garden, the peach house repaired, the vinery dismantled and the pipes sold off. A new glasshouse was built by Mackenzie and Moncur of Edinburgh and the orchard outside the wall planted up with 300 apple trees from Dickson's of Waterloo Place, Edinburgh.

To link House of Falkland to the palace, he asked David Storrar, a local architect from Cupar, to construct the Palace Walk in 1890. This begins at a gate in the west side of the palace wall and crosses the Maspie Burn into the newly planted orchard. A bridge was built to span the ancient road running into Falkland, between high retaining walls, linking it to the elevated riverbank. Stone was brought from local quarries and the whole works were to cost £373. For just under a mile the walk then follows the north side of the burn past the back of the stables and on up to the house over another bridge. Edward Sang & Sons of Kirkcaldy supplied flowering shrubs and plants for the landscaping in March 1891. There were over 300 rhododendrons, golden elders, weigelias, skimmias, daphnes, sweet briars, *clematis montana* and *hydrangea paniculata* to give a variety of flowering throughout the year.

Not content with the existing interiors at the House of Falkland, which may have looked old fashioned after 50 years, Bute initially consulted William Frame, who had worked on a number of his other projects, to completely remodel the inside of House of Falkland and add a chapel. Bute dismissed Frame in October 1890 on finding him drunk in the local inn, replacing him with Robert Weir Schultz who had just started working at St John's Lodge, London. Bringing in Schultz at this stage clearly influenced how the landscape would be embellished too.

Along with the complete remodelling of the house, Schultz began by developing the pond in front of the stables. At the east road entrance to the estate from the town is a small gate lodge with the Mill Burn running behind it. Schultz created a charming fishpond, framed by stone parapets at each end, the lower where the burn cascades down and under an extension to the lodge, the higher on a stone bridge with a more ornamental cascade under it. It was stocked with two-year old trout. He built an oak tree seat, recently remade, and similar to the one at St John's Lodge, under a lime tree on the grass. He designed two new garden buildings. The Buckie House, a round summerhouse on the north side of the Maspie Burn in Scroggie Park near the cricket pitch, survived until the 1970s. With its shell-lined ceiling and wrought iron gates with the initials J and G, it was demolished to its foundations. On the rising ground to the south of the main house was a rectangular summerhouse, which has also

Pond designed by Weir-Schultz with new tree bench in 2005.

not survived. Both ornamental structures were built by Robert Miller, the estate joiner, and thatched either with reeds or heather, a traditional estate practice.

Schultz also enhanced the plantings around the stables, the pond and the Palace Walk to a plan approved by the Marquess in 1893. A new circular walk was developed, too, from the pond bridge through the park and up to the house. Box plants from this period still survive amongst the trees. Because strong plants are specified, it appears that some of the initial planting along the Palace Walk needed to be supplemented. Similar kinds of flowering shrubs to the original plantings were ordered, including another 450 rhododendrons, exotic trees like scarlet American oaks and purple beech, and climbers such as clematis, honeysuckles, roses

Thatched
summerhouse.
Late nineteenth
century.

and six Chinese wisterias. Three latticed rose arches for the walk were made by John Birrell, the blacksmith. A contemporary postcard shows climbing roses on the entrance lodge and an account allows for wiring being put on the walls of the house by "Lady Margaret's garden". Further specific bills indicate that John Patrick's daughter took a keen interest in her garden, ordering snowdrops, crocus, narcissi, anemones and scillas. In 1896 the parterres, around the house, were being bedded up with hundreds of tulips, hyacinths, snowdrops, daffodils and narcissi.

While the lower gardens were being enhanced, the area of woodland leading to and around the temple on Greenhill was also being extensively developed. Firstly a tall stone bridge, with balustrade, was built over the Maspie Burn beside the house, by John Fernie, the mason. This was to enable direct access from the west of the house across the burn while still allowing the original picturesque walk up the Maspie Den to continue underneath. A new walk referred to as the "Gilderland walk to the pine woods from Falkland house", after the wife of James II, Mary of Guilderland, was created. Its name was a romantic reference to the royal history of the palace and landscape, which had been given to Mary as a marriage settlement in 1449. A long straight beech hedge was planted passing between two small copses, also named the Queen's Quarrels, to join up to the circular walks, newly under-planted with rhododendrons and flowering shrubs, which climbed up through the trees *en route* to the temple. A number of other 'signature' beech hedges remain from this period throughout the estate. The use of beech was likely to have been influenced by Dumfries House, where beech hedging is very much part of the wider landscape.

For the walk the blacksmith produced iron seats in 1897 and a metal bower, which may be the one still spanning the path. John Patrick was not keen on riding, preferring to walk everywhere, and the height of this bower on the Gilderland Walk suggests that it really was intended for pedestrians, not riders. For luncheon parties at the temple, Robert Miller made an oak table and a dozen chairs and elaborate new decorations, including red glass in the roof, were executed.

John Patrick was a very keen curler along with his sons John and Ninian. In 1896 labourers dug out a curling pond beside the orchard near the palace and puddled clay for the lining. A clubhouse, designed by Schultz, was built by William Page and thatched with reeds cut at Newburgh near the river Tay. One room was for players and the other for the Bute family. Though the rink has now become a bowling green, the house still remains with a pantiled roof.

When John Patrick died in 1900, his second son, Lord Ninian, who inherited the estate, was not yet of age. A painting of him standing in a kilt alongside his mother celebrating his majority in 1904 hangs in the old library of the palace. Lord Ninian married the Hon. Ismay Preston, daughter of Viscount Gormanston, in 1906. They had two sons and two daughters. The following year the family started to spend more time at Falkland.

Westfield Bridge with the Maspie Den walk running through it, 2008.

A gun room was fitted at the house in 1908, and the stables, with its new clock tower, accommodated Lord Ninian's racehorses, but was also partly converted for cars. A magnificent round metal horse trough made in Glasgow in 1911, recently restored, took centre stage. A Swiss Pine, *Pinus cembra*, was planted in front of a new chapel on a knoll above the fishpond and in direct line between the house and the town church. It was intended as a Catholic church for the parish. Reginald Fairlie, a friend and neighbour of Myres Castle, was the young architect commissioned to design it. Work began in 1912 using stone quarried nearby. It was never finished and remains a memorial to Lord Ninian, killed in action at Loos, France, in 1915, and his infant son Ringan, who died in 1910. It continues as a family burial ground.

Michael Crichton Stuart inherited the estate and keepership of the palace as a baby on the death of his father, spending the holidays with his mother and sisters at House of Falkland. During the First World War it was run as a convalescent home for injured officers by Ismay Crichton-Stuart. She later married Captain Maule Ramsay, one of her patients, and produced four more sons. The estate continued to be managed by the factor, George Gavin. After the family left to live permanently at Kellie Castle, Angus, in 1927, the house continued to be used solely for shooting parties, until Second World War, with informal grouse shoots on

Curling pavilion and
rink. Early twentieth
century.

the hills, partridge in the fields next to the house and pheasants in the woods. Gamekeepers
continued until 1980.

Conifer forest planting continued on the estate following the compulsory purchase
order of trees for the First World War war effort and the harvesting of other mature timber.
During the Second World War Polish officers were billeted at the house and the estate was
used to train members of the Free Polish army, so it was not until after the war that Michael,
now a major in the Scots Guards, could return to Falkland with his wife Barbara to take up the
management of the estate. Injuries sustained during the war meant that he was unable to walk
great distances, and so his interest in Falkland focused on the palace where they decided to live.

The living quarters were therefore expanded and modernised for the couple to
reside in with their young family and House of Falkland was leased out to tenants as a school.
The parterre was grassed over and retained only its pyramidal yews and fountains to recall
its former glory while the vases, plinths and urns were stored away for safety. From the First
World War the palace grounds had been dug up and used as a tree nursery and subsequently
leased out as a market garden. A crop of potatoes was used to clean the ground after the
Second World War with the promise of a new initiative. In 1940 the orchard beside the palace
had been replanted. Now that the Keeper was living permanently at the palace Percy Cane,
the well-known garden architect, was asked to design a garden within the palace walls in 1947.

Cane's career had become notable in the 1930s through two publications *My
Garden Illustrated* and *Garden Design*. He had created gardens for Hailie Selassie in Ethiopia
and at the British Pavilion, World's Fair, New York in 1939, as well as at Ardencraig, Isle of
Bute, for Lord Colum Crichton-Stuart, Michael's uncle. Cane came up with the concept of
a "garden glade", which was described as a "harmony of plant and stone", by Arthur Hellyer.
"I think of it as a formalised woodland... an attempt to combine the orderliness and firm outline
characteristic of formal gardens with the... flowing line and pictorial charm of the landscape
style", Cane wrote.

Firstly Cane wanted to enhance the palace setting by emphasising its architectural features without hiding or detracting from them. To do this he planted columnar cypresses at regular intervals on the highest level, the east terrace, with a flagged walk. He felt that the descending slopes, surrounded by walls, were monotonous in their unvaried greens when viewed from the palace windows. To overcome this monotony he designed the pleasure grounds, linked from the palace and its ruined foundations by new steps, with a central glade. Along the whole length of the green sward were six half-moon shaped beds of mixed trees and shrubs while contrasting long herbaceous borders hugged the line of the walls. A number of existing trees were removed, while others were kept to give maturity to the scheme. The curving island beds were planted with cherry, philadelphus, weigela, ceanothus and cytisus, their shape and height offering a foil to the straight herbaceous walks.

Michael Crichton
Stuart.

Bill Jenkins, the head gardener, planted the flowerbed below the west terrace, the lupin border, with the salmon and yellow Bessie Darling Inglis and Russell hybrids, which toned with overhanging climbing roses. It was renowned in its time. Facing south, on the same level and overlooked from the north terrace, Cane choose hotter colours for contrast: scarlet poppies, the crimson monarda Cambridge Scarlet with purple salvias, blue and purple delphiniums and yellow and orange heliopsis. A blue border with a flower scheme of soft pink, mauve, grey, blue and white was created near to the remains of the twelfth century castle which John Patrick had had excavated. Another great long border against the outside east palace wall was planted up for easier maintenance with groups of perennials planted

Lupin border at
Falkland Palace,
designed by Percy
Cane in 1947.

amongst flowering shrubs, some chosen for their foliage. There was a peony walk and an iris border too. At the farthest end from the palace Cane kept two large urns, originally from House of Falkland.

In the lower garden in front of the royal tennis court Cane produced a design of two ponds connected by a rill. This was never carried out. Instead its concept was partially adopted by Euan Cox who filled the raised ponds he designed in 1955 with water lilies and yellow irises, flagging the spaces in between and planting horizontal junipers.

In 1952 Michael arranged for the National Trust for Scotland to take on the deputy keepership ensuring the long-term management of the palace and its gardens and provided an endowment by selling his Durham estates. Preparation was made to open to the public and as part of this ongoing process the Information centre, designed by Schomberg Scott, with its herb garden and draughts set were created in 1965.

Over the last forty years a slow process of change developed in gardening the palace and inevitably some of Cane's original planting plans were altered. Delphiniums were substituted for lupins in the border. A refurbishment of the garden in 1978, though not changing the basic layout, resulted in losing historically important cultivars of herbaceous plants. The Russian vine, which frothed over the tower at the end of the east range, was removed because of fear of damage to the structure. Dark green cypressas were planted along the walls, contrasting with the remaining four paler, thinner originals. With a new head gardener, Sonia Ferras-Mana, the

Trust's plan is to gradually restore the garden to Cane's design intentions, removing some trees, reshaping the maturing shrubs, but retaining the delphiniums in the lupin border because it has proved impossible to find the original varieties.

The wider wooded landscape of House of Falkland was replanted, as was the practice after the Second World War, with commercial conifers, and in 1955 a plaque was unveiled by Barbara Crichton Stuart at the Bruce monument: "To mark the centenary of the laird who first afforested the Lomonds, to the great benefit of his country in two world wars; also to record a season during which 140 acres have been replanted...."

Palace from the Iris Pool, c. 1950.

Falkland Palace, with cypresses used by Percy Cane to emphasize the architectural features of the building.

A storm in 1968 felled many trees in the dressed ground beside the house and with a subsequent replanting with conifers in 1980 the sheer density of commercial plantings inevitably changed the rhythm and picturesque nature of the woods, which had been a careful mixture of broadleaved and exotics trees under-planted with flowering shrubs. A monkey puzzle and a sequoia, Victorian plantings, poking above the woods remind us of their former glory.

Michael died in 1981 leaving stewardship to his son Ninian, who returned in the early 1990s to grapple with this neglected work of art in slow decay. A Heritage Lottery funding in 2002 allowed for a comprehensive programme of essential repair work on the bridges, paths, and structure of the designed landscape of Maspie Den. There is free access to the public throughout the estate with 70,000 visits a year. Volunteers continue to help tree plant, clear and manage the woods, and slowly it is hoped that in the twenty-first century the landscape will recover its former beauty.

A new walk was created from the edge of Scroggie Park to the Pillars of Hercules, based on a lost nineteenth century path, enabling access for walkers and the disabled all the way from the burgh to an organic farm shop, over an old quarry bridge, without using the main road. Inspired by a dream, it was completed in 2005. A drystone wall alongside was restored and a litany in Scots written into the walls by the Scottish letter cutters. The theme *solvitur ambulando*—solved by walking—in an unconscious way builds on John Patrick's love of walking and reflection within the landscape.

Standin, thinking, danderin.... plowtering, pondering dreaming, ... bein.

Ninian Crichton Stuart clearing vegetation in the woodlands of Falkland.

From John Patrick's exclusive Victorian retreat, 150 years later, his great grandson, Ninian is committed to a policy of enterprising stewardship involving the revival of the estate, not just as a work of art but as a fruitful working landscape, which sustains people and maintains income flow. To this date over 15 kilometers, about ten miles, of the original nineteenth century path networks have been restored echoing the original vision.

Dumfries House

North side of
Dumfries House
from the flood plain,
2008.

Dumfries House is an exquisitely proportioned and restrained Palladian building resting on the lip of a bowl in the winding valley of the River Lugar close to Cumnock in Ayrshire. With its back elevation overlooking the valley and its front facing south towards a long gentle upward slope, its setting is the inspired outcome of discussions in 1736 between the father of the 5th Earl of Dumfries, Colonel Dalrymple, husband of Penelope, Countess of Dumfries in her own right, and William Adam, builder and architect, who had had much experience in advising other Scottish landowners. These included the Earl of Stair, Dalrymple's elder brother, for whom Adam had accomplished landscaping improvements on his estates at Newliston and Castle Kennedy and who would have recommended him for this commission. For over 100 years the Dumfries family had been occupying the fifteenth century Liefnorris House lower down the slope at the edge of the flood plain. On inheriting, the 5th Earl of Dumfries commissioned the sons of William Adam to design the new house, in 1748, with Robert assuming particular responsibility.

The grounds would seem to have been already planted up by Penelope, the 5th Earl's mother. A number of large roundels of trees appear on General Roy's map of 1750, notably the one called Stair and another named Dettingen after the battle fought in 1743 against the French in what is now Germany. William had been aide de camp to his uncle, Earl of Stair, the nominal commander in chief. Rewards from this victory could have helped to finance this new house. These particular roundels are divided into unequal wedges with a central circular clearing and distinct lines of view radiating outwards. Of over five acres in area and originally planted with beech, they are still defined by surprisingly wide stone rubble walls. They have been considered as representing the troop positions at Dettingen but it is more likely that they were named simply in memory of the event as a proper account has never been established of this battle, the last in which a reigning British monarch took part.

Roy's map also delineates avenues of trees: on the main road to Ayr, along the estate road eastwards to Auchinleck and notably one running north through Pennyland from the river ford immediately opposite the new house site. Trees obscured easterly views from

Previous pages:
Cattle drinking in
the River Lugar.
Behind them is
the Adam bridge,
beyond which can be
seen the Lady's Well,
also designed by
John Adam. Detail
of painting by Jacob
Thompson, 1837.

the house towards the remains of the fifteenth century Tarringzean castle on its outcrop of rocks overlooking the Lugar. On suddenly being revealed to visitors it would have engendered surprise as well as lending an important picturesque element to the landscape and an authenticity of age when landowners elsewhere were building mock ruins for such effects. A charming restored dovecote from 1671 and a farm steading were already in place. The old gardens around Liefnorris were swept away while a walled kitchen garden was being established several hundred yards to the west on land falling steeply southwards to the river, with an orchard planted on the side closest to the house. Moving the house to a new site proved an ideal opportunity to create utility gardens some distance away, following a trend in Scotland at the time of locating kitchen and walled gardens away from the homes they served.

Although work had started the previous year to drain the site and establish the foundations of Dumfries House, a house party assembled on 18 July 1754 to celebrate the laying of the first stone above ground. Tents were pitched for the reception, musicians played, and in the evening lamps were lit in the trees. The whole ceremony culminated in a ball. Robert Adam was just about to leave on his tour of Italy, which was to inspire him to create his best known works, most of them in England. He received the first down-payment of £1,500. The total cost of the house was to come in at its estimate of £7,979, 11 shillings and twopence. Habitable by 1759, the house was made with timber from the estate and blue freestone dragged from local quarries by oxen. Internal stucco work by Clayton, who had worked on other Adam projects and considerable fine furnishings bought from Chippendale complemented the Gobelins tapestries, originally acquired by the Earl of Stair to whom they had been presented by Louis XIV when he was ambassador to France. The project throughout was over-seen, rather surprisingly, by the gardener, Robert Neilson.

To serve as gateway and lodges for the principal estate entrance drive from the north, the imposing Temple was designed by John Adam, then running the building business in Scotland. An elaborate eye catcher in Gothic style, it is built of red sandstone on an elevated setting at the boundary of the estate which is defined by a ha-ha. Two half-roundels of trees were already planted on each side. As part of the same dramatic, scenic approach, a high stone bridge was erected over the Lugar, downstream from the ford, with a pair of obelisks on each side and balustrades capped with balls. The changing views from the drive formed an integral part of the landscape plan as the house should only have been glimpsed through carefully contrived planting until the carriages had crossed the bridge, driven up the incline and swept round into the south entrance court. Legal preparation had failed to keep pace with engineering progress, however, and this grand scheme did not achieve the effect which was intended. William failed to secure the right-of-way over his neighbour's land and the gateway was never to be used except as a folly. Bitter arguments ensued for years with the Boswell family and, by the time the disputed land was eventually brought into the estate in the next century, the will no longer existed to use the Temple for its intended purpose.

With the thwarting of its use as the principal entrance drive, other entrances were to be created. Two pairs of single storey lodges were built on the Ayr road to the south, one pair at West Gates, and the other further east at Stockiehill, where the house was approached over Lady's Bridge. Adam's bridge continued in use as a river crossing but was deprived of its

Adam Temple.
Mid-twentieth
century.

main motive, being far too grand to simply serve the kitchen garden. Later in the nineteenth century yet another entrance drive was opened from the village of Cumnock passing close to Tarringzean castle and up through a beech avenue.

Drinking water flowed along elm pipes from a spring at Milzeoch, two miles south, to a tank in Cistern Mount, a small clump of trees near the Ayr road. From here it continued to the house where lead piping was installed by Robert Selby, the plumber, along with two water closets, which may have been linked with a large culvert still running from the house down into the flood plain. Selby also plumbed up the new washhouse nearby from its own internal well, covered with a wooden lid. John Adam designed a number of other ancillary works including the Lady's Well next to the river beyond the bleaching green, which may have replaced a previous small conical building. With no spring to service the well, its function was probably just ornamental. An icehouse, used in the twentieth century as a game larder, was set in some trees not far from the new house. A stable with six stalls and a classic five-door coach house, harled and painted, was built near the old house and by the next year the Adams' work was completed. Leifnorris was eventually demolished in 1771 and beech trees planted on its site.

The Earl's business interests helped to fund estate improvements. He exploited opportunities to sell cattle to England and to supply wool, flax and leather for shipment to America from ports on the Clyde while he laid out an octagonal bowling green in Shaw Wood east of the house. Cut into the slope and circled by yew trees, it formed part of a new east-west axis from the house and is still discernible today. New rides were made through this wood and limes and other trees planted. Conifers, acting as nurse trees on the mounts and elsewhere, were grubbed up as the broadleaved trees developed.

There had been a walled garden and house at Waterside since 1750. In 1766 the local mason surrounded a new, extended kitchen garden with a wall 12 feet high, in brick with flat stone copings and two gateways to the north and east. The side from which visitors would approach was faced in stone. As centrepiece to the walled garden stands today a fine old sycamore tree, described already in 1911 as "the oldest living thing in Cumnock." It must have been of particular bearing to be retained in the new kitchen garden. On the north wall was a hot house heated at one time by tan bark brought from Auchinleck. A large bank of quarried stone was raised to protect the south wall fronting the river from the turbulence of waters in spate.

William died in 1768 and the estate passed to his nephew, Patrick Macdowell, a grandson of Penelope, who adopted her family name of Crichton. Tree planting and the draining and enclosing of land continued apace during his stewardship with one man alone being responsible for 20 miles of stone dykes and 40 miles of hedging. Large banks were built along both sides of the river below the house to protect against flood waters which can

Adam Bridge
in 1905.

rise rapidly by up to ten feet. The bridge had been well designed against water damage with parapet splays of unusual width opening onto the northern bank. A path cresting that bank was named Lord Dumfries' Walk. A nine foot stone ha-ha defined the west boundary of the estate along the edge of Humeston Wood, lined inside with three rows of trees and a straight walk. One row of fine tall beech trees on the very edge of the wall now threatens its stability. A circular picturesque gravelled walk crossing two small bridges over Polcalk Burn was created for Elizabeth, Patrick's daughter, in Polcalk Wood, to the south of the Ayr road, through trees under-planted with shrubs.

His gardener David Patton, heading a full-time staff of eight, was particularly keen to acquire new kinds of gooseberries from Edinburgh. He writes: "Mr J Gordon of Fountainbridge is possessed of 19 kinds of fruits and is the only person in Scotland that is able to give ane assortment of good kinds..." and to identify them he had: "some thin sheet lead numbers to be nailed upon garden wall in order to preserve the true names of the different kinds of fruit... names may be known by one single inspection." A new hothouse was built in

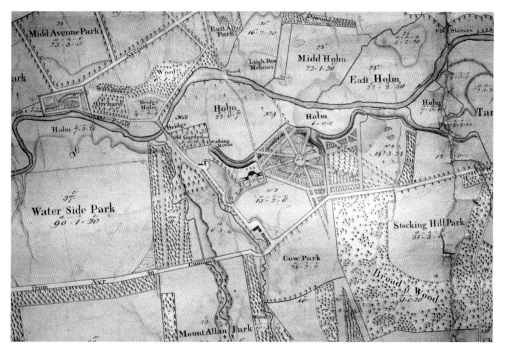

1772 plan of Dumfries Estate by John Home. Shaw Wood just east of the house with its rides radiating from a central octagonal bowling green and the walled kitchen garden to the north west beside the river show up prominently.

the walled garden and the old one removed in 1783, while later John Morton, the mason in Cumnock, made an *equinoidal* sundial.

William had begun employing three men to extract minerals at Garlaff nearby in 1767. Patrick continued this initiative by installing a steam engine at the mine to pump out water to allow for deeper working of the pit. Coal was supplied to Dumfries House and hothouse, to tenants' homes, to mills for drying grain and to the lime kilns at Benston. Consignments of coal for shipment from Ayr were constrained by the conditions of the road until the railways were laid in the 1850s. James Taylor, the inventor of steam navigation who had been born nearby, reported on the mineralogical prospects of the estate for Patrick but the coal enterprises failed to expand at this time.

In 1790, Patrick was elected a Representative Peer of Scotland and would have come to London to attend the House of Lords with his daughter, Lady Elizabeth Crichton, where it is possible that she met the son of the 1st Marquess of Bute, Lord Mountstuart. Although there had been talk of his marrying Frances Coutts, daughter of the rich London banker, Elizabeth's prospects and person proved of even greater attraction to him. They were married and rapidly produced an heir, John. Protracted negotiations over the marriage settlement and a subsequent court case between the Crichtons and the Stuarts were still ongoing when Mountstuart died from falling off his horse in 1794. Another son, James, was born posthumously. Elizabeth, too, died soon after. In 1803 the orphaned John Stuart became the 7th Earl of Dumfries on the death of Patrick, his grandfather, later appending his mother's surname, Crichton, to his own.

Until he came of age in 1814, a number of Trustees were put in charge of running the estate, including the Earl of Dalkeith and Mr Crawford Tait, a lawyer. The forester at Dumfries House was immediately sacked on grounds of dishonesty and Gilbert Ross, head gardener for 24 years, took over his duties while the trustees looked for a replacement. Management of

Detail: 6th Earl of Dumfries with Flora Countess of Loudon by Henry Raeburn, 1793.

the kitchen garden was rationalised. Its produce went to servants, labourers and pensioners while parts were put down to grass. Instructions were given to "... practice what the late Earl did in cutting down trees so as not to lose anything of utility or beauty in the plantations... not to cut any wood for sale except if tenants need it for mending fences." A sawmill was duly erected on the Backburn, restricted by water flow to winter use. With foresight the trustees purchased land adjoining the estate when it became available. By 1809 over £65,000 had been spent on 11 lots from the Ochiltree estate to the west. The Marquess of Bute attended meetings and suggested further land purchase and improvements in drainage to increase the income derived from rents. Developments in the mines continued and a contract was made with Messrs MacAdam & Sons to supply black lead but the enterprise was still not lucrative.

Painting of the walled garden with view to Dumfries House by Jacob Thomson, 1830.

Detail: Lady Elizabeth Crichton with her mother the Countess of Dumfries by Henry Raeburn, 1793.

John came of age the same year that he became the 2nd Marquess of Bute, uniting the estates of the Dumfries and Bute families with the Cardiff estates of the Windsor family and those in Durham. Though John had lived at Dumfries House as a child with his mother, he now only used it for occasional visits, having a large number of other properties to oversee. Both grandfathers had passed on to him their sense of duty and enthusiasm for good, active land management and he took his role very seriously. The Waterloo bridge, named in honour of his close friend, the Duke of Wellington, was built at the mouth of the Backburn where it enters the Lugar so that a walk could be made into the newly acquired Ochiltree lands. After his marriage to Maria North the kitchen garden was put back to full production, with greater emphasis placed on its ornamental potential since there was no other flower garden at the house. The glasshouse was built into the bank in the middle of the kitchen garden and from its balustraded terrace, adorned with a sundial, came fine views extending to the house.

John knew that the estate's interest and that of the tenants were linked. The tenants could collect shoe tiles from his works at Ochiltree with no charge as long as they drained a minimum number of acres each year by digging 21 inch furrows and laying them at their own expense, as similarly happened on his Cardiff estates. He also encouraged dairy farming by patronising the local farmer's association which awarded prizes for different categories of Ayrshire milk cows. As a consequence, by the end of the century, dairy cattle dominated the pastureland while sheep grazed the moors. When improvements were made to the road to Ayr in the 1840s, which included shifting it further to the south of Dumfries House the Stockiehill gatehouses were denied their function and left stranded in the landscape.

On John's sudden death in 1848, his brother James, resident at Cardiff Castle, moved to Dumfries House with his large family while awaiting the settlement of the estates. Within the provisions of the law, as next-of-kin, he was in charge of managing the Scottish estates. Tensions with his brother's second wife, Sophia, initially prevented her and her infant son living there. Nevertheless, the 3rd Marquess did spend time at Dumfries House later on as a child, both with his mother and with Lady Elizabeth Moore. After 1866 when his Scottish

Parterre garden to the south of the house with its original pink gravel. It is thought to have been inspired by the interlocking squares and circles of Byzantine church architecture.

guardians, Sir James and Lady Ferguson, occupied the house, he would visit occasionally, always calling it his homeliest of houses.

On his coming of age the landscape was to change. In 1872 a branch line of the Glasgow and South Western railway was opened south of the main road to which the estate's own station was connected by a straight approach flanked by a row of wellingtonias, *Sequoia gigantea*, and other exotic conifers beside Lady Elizabeth's Walk. Many more wellingtonias, North American firs and several copper beech were planted, often in uneven rows, throughout the policies: beside the river, beyond Waterloo Bridge, at the Cumnock entrance lodge, near the kitchen garden and around the stables, without any explicit design intention. Though contrasting with the native broadleaved woodlands, they have now grown into stately specimens. In particular the wellingtonia nearest to the house has uncharacteristically retained its lowest branches which, skirting the ground, give it an imperiously stately air.

The Butes spent Christmas of 1877 at Dumfries House while recovering from the shock of the fire at Mount Stuart and, for some time thereafter, it became their principal home in Scotland. Immediately after New Year, excavations were made in front of the house by the gardeners to implement their employer's design, an unusual sunken grass parterre combining interlocking squares and circles, inspired by Byzantine church architecture. He had learnt to appreciate such ecclesiastical patterns on his sailing trips around the eastern Mediterranean. "These churches are, it is true, invariably on the plan of a fat + inscribed in a square"... he wrote later. The garden, when viewed from above, assumes the ground plan of an idealised Greek church but also resembles the St Sophia church at Tsarskoe Selo near St Petersburg, which John Patrick had also visited. The centre of each circle was a flowerbed surrounded by pink ash, with steps down to the middle where a bronze statue stood. This statue was one of the many souvenirs from his travels with which John Patrick used to decorate his houses and gardens. A statue of Mercury and two copies of ancient Greek athletes from Pompeii, acquired in Naples, were placed in front of the house. A number of new walks, also spread with ash, snaked through the woods, ran beside the river or proceeded north towards Auchinleck church. Trees were planted to soften the views towards the south river bank. Although few remain, the limes which formed the fine avenue along the north bank are still an important feature.

John Patrick and his sons enjoyed curling on their rink at Woodhead in the severe winter of 1894–1895. Robert Weir Schultz, working at St John's Lodge and House of Falkland, came to stay and amused everybody by tobogganing down a snowy slope on a tea-tray. His first addition to the garden in front of the house was the design of two flowerbeds for the side lawns; he then squared off the sunken garden to enhance his client's parterre scheme. All the beds had to be permanently netted with three foot chicken wire as protection from rabbits. In addition to his plans to extend the house behind the arcades of the Adam wings, Schultz also designed New Chiswick, called after the famous house in London which John Patrick had leased before St John's Lodge. This was a woodland garden with an orchard to the west of

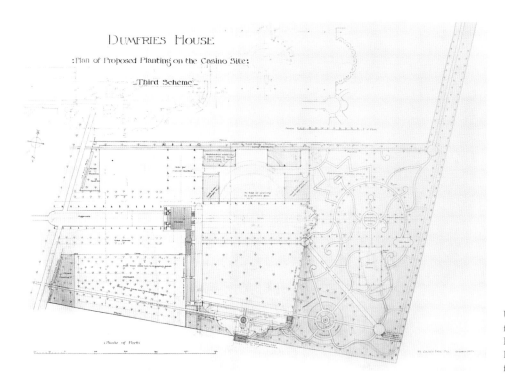

Unrealised proposal for a scheme at Dumfries House by Robert Weir Schultz from 1893.

Humeston Wood, in what was then a large field. Lying on the east-west axis, this would serve to balance Shaw Wood and the old bowling green, now overgrown with trees, on the other side of the house. Trees were cleared in Humeston to allow a site line from the house to New Chiswick, extending into the garden's central pathway. Entrances were opened through the nine foot dyke, separating Humeston from the field, and on one was fitted three foot curved double gates fashioned in oak. A porticoed orangery was planned and a well was dug. Work carried out on this garden at considerable expense over three years came to an end in 1900 when John Patrick died after a prolonged illness. At his request, a memorial was erected at the place of his death. A full-size marble cross designed by Nathaniel Westlake, bearing a figure of Christ, overlooks the Lugar from a steep eminence at the edge of Shaw Woods with an inscription reading "Thy wounds are my merits" and recreates in three dimensions the art of Caspar David Friedrich.

Schultz was kept on by John, the 4th Marquess, to pursue the architectural alterations to the house although his plans for a Chinese bridge over the Lugar, where an iron bridge had been, and for the orangery in New Chiswick were never realised. The remnants of that garden are just one pair of Schultz's oak gates leading into a field so that it is hard to imagine now that there was any designed landscape there at all.

Initially John used Dumfries House largely as a shooting lodge. This was the estate where he and his brother, Ninian, had first shot game under the supervision of a gamekeeper in 1894. The rabbit problem had become so dire that in 1905 over 1,000 of the pests were shot during a three week period. John's great success, however, was the development of the grouse moors at Kyle and Dalblair which he took to managing personally, supervising the arrangement of the butts, the drainage of the land and burning of the heather. This led to an increase in the annual bag from 100 to 3,000 brace of birds and in some years even more. The weight of grouse meat represented as much as half the sheep meat over the same stretch of moorland.

Later Dumfries House was where John's growing family of seven children could keep all their ponies at the stables while he devised landscape improvements for the estate. One involved re-instating the principal drive from Auchinleck through the Temple as originally envisaged and moving the bridge upstream to a point opposite the house from where the drive would divide and run up the slope on either side of the house to curl round and meet at the front door. Ornamental Highland, Galloway and Dexter cattle were to graze and grace the fields in front of the house. The old well-head designed by Adam, close to the site of the

Cross to commemerate the 3rd Marquess.

former house, was to be transferred to where there actually was a spring. All such projects were abandoned after the First World War as worries about the debt burden to his heirs of death duties made John decide to dispose of both the Dumfries and Cardiff estates.

A variation to that plan was considered, however, in 1924, by which 35,000 acres, over half the Dumfries estate, would be sold to the sitting tenant farmers and the mining rights leased to William Baird of Dalmellington. By the end of the nineteenth century the coalmines had become the main employer in the Cumnock area, developed by the 2nd Marquess with his experience of mining in South Wales and Durham. Excavation was excluded from 300 yards around the house but this did not prevent subsidence to nearby property. In the 1960s the Coal Board was obliged to completely repair the Adam bridge using a concrete beam and

South side of house in 1950. The symmetry and dignity of the elevation remain unchanged today.

later pay compensation to the 6th Marquess when safety measures forced him to dismantle parts of the crumbling Temple.

During the Second World War a prisoner of war camp was built at Pennyland north of the river. British officers, billeted in the house, destroyed the Lady's Well by using it as target practice from the rifle range at the back of the house. Its remains have only recently been cleared. From 1957 Eileen, widow of the 5th Marquess, an advocate of Palladian elegance, resided permanently in the house, the first time in 150 years that any member of the family had done so. She occupied herself with breeding race horses and gardening, looking after the small burn garden at the bottom of Lady Elizabeth's Walk with its Victorian peach house, since demolished. The kitchen garden was leased to Jim Gillian who sold the produce while his wife kept a pretty garden on the bank outside. The old laundry was converted to accommodating students who came to help out on the estate.

The 6th Marquess chose to rent out the grouse moors, ranked amongst the finest in Scotland under the aegis of the 4th Marquess. In 1974 over 5,000 brace were shot but from the 1980s numbers have declined, aggravated by disease of the grouse, over-grazing by sheep and poor heather management with depredation by the heather beetle. In 1981 Muirkirk Uplands became a Site of Special Scientific Interest (SSSI) for its important upland and blanket bog habitat and numbers of hen harriers and short-eared owls. Scottish Natural Heritage is keen to increase bio-diversity. By careful livestock control, a mosaic of different plant species should give cover for a greater variety of smaller birds like skylarks and pipits to nest and provide food for predators like the hen harriers. The Dumfries estate shoot is part of this SSSI as well as of a Special Protection Area, a European directive under which hen harriers are protected.

Mid-twentieth century commercial plantings and the Cumnock bypass, which severed Tarringzean castle from the rest of the policies, have diminished the picturesque

Children of the
4th Marquess on
horseback outside
Dumfries House,
c. 1920.

nature of the landscape. This may be partially reversed, however, as the conifers are harvested and replaced with broadleaved woods, some from natural regeneration. Since 1993 and the death of both Eileen and her son, the 6th Marquess, the future of the 20,000 acre estate has been in question and the house shut up. John, the 7th Marquess, like his great-grandfather, has a more commercial approach to his estates. The stone balls which decorated the bridge and statues from the front of the house were stored, for fear of theft or vandalism, while the future of the house was decided. The kitchen garden lies sadly unused. Even the nature of mineral extraction has changed with open cast mining replacing the deep mines, all of which had closed by 1990.

Drive to the
kitchen garden with
gardener's house,
c. 1920.

In 2007 the house and contents were sold. John had never felt the same passion for Dumfries House as he has for Mount Stuart, considering it rather as his grandmother's home. Ever since its ownership by the Butes it has always been of lesser importance and interest to the family than Mount Stuart, and John prefers to live a simpler life from his forebears. Though the house was offered to the National Trust for Scotland after Eileen's death and negotiations were recently revived, it was in June 2007 that the Prince of Wales stepped in to guarantee a sizeable loan which enabled the House to be procured for the benefit of the Nation. In the twenty-first century for the first time the public will be able to enjoy visiting Dumfries House and Robert Adam's restrained elegance and in time the landscape, which his father William helped to inspire, will be restored.

Old Place of Mochrum

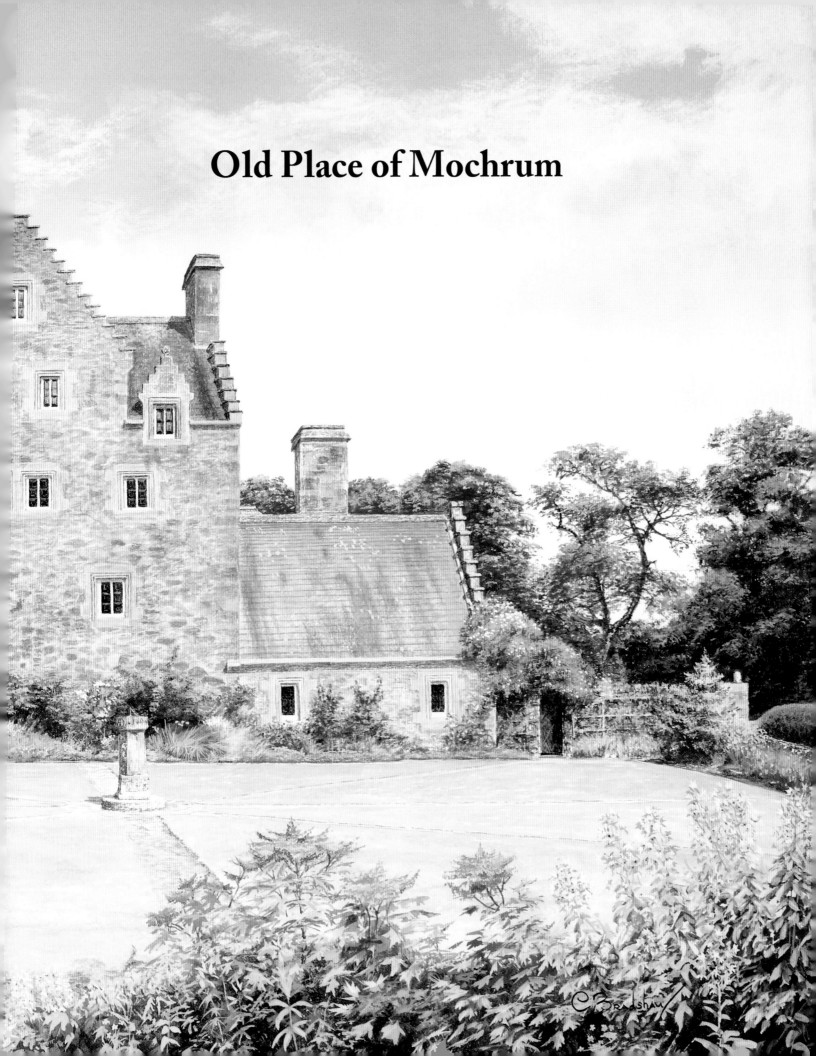

Detail of Old Place from 1790 survey for the 6th Earl of Dumfries.

Previous pages: Contemporary view of the garden of Old Place at Mochrum. Watercolour by Graham Bradshaw. Early twenty-first century.

Old Place and its estate of 16,500 acres lies on a remote open moor, scattered with small lochs, in the Machars region of Galloway in the south-west of Scotland. With its wild and lonely setting it resembles no other Bute landscape. The name Mochrum means 'hill in the plain by the sea' in old Celtic. Even though Whithorn to the south was the earliest recorded Christian community in Scotland, founded by St Ninian, the isolated Machars had become a lawless place in the fifteenth century, leading to the need for a fortified house. It was renamed 'Old Place' when the owner built a new house, Mochrum Park, 12 miles away. Colonel William Dalrymple of the Stair family acquired it in 1738 and it came to the Butes by descent through his marriage with Penelope, Countess of Dumfries, in 1698. Of its two rectangular towers, the older one to the west with its four storeys, parapets and five and a half foot thick walls was built from 1474 by Sir John Dunbar. It was later connected by a high wall to the south tower, of similar height but with a simpler roof treatment. A courtyard was created by the addition of a range on the two remaining sides. In 1718 a hole had to be broken in one of the tower walls to lower Sir James Dunbar's coffin, owing to his great size. Stone walls enclosed both the orchard to the north of the house and the south garden which, because of the sloping land, was buttressed on its south and east sides. Its name 'place' and the existence of external walled enclosures suggested that it ceased to be a house with the need to be defended with fortifications.

Political stability in Scotland in the second half of the eighteenth century, coupled with the general advance in agricultural knowledge throughout the United Kingdom, encouraged local landowners to make improvements to their estates and the quality of their

Survey of Mochrum estate, 1790.

GRAY

Loch
Hempton

M.Doual's
Loch

PARKHILLS

Mochrum
Place

Challochglen
Glenoour

Mill
well

Ruins of a Castle

Loch

of

DRUMWALT

GRAY.

Mochrum

livestock. Large numbers of black cattle were driven south to be fattened for the London market and it was said that drovers preferred animals with a white belt so that their whereabouts could be seen in the dark. From 1776 when Port William was founded on the coast five miles south of Old Place, cattle as well as sheep, oats and potatoes could be shipped to Liverpool. At this time Patrick, Earl of Dumfries, the 2nd Marquess' grandfather, started planting considerable clumps of trees wherever suitable on his land, encouraging his tenants to do so too. Few trees survived, however, some being burnt in the early 1800s when tenant John McGeoch set fire to the heather and allowed it to get out of hand. A report from 1857 describes the area as barren and mossy. A lack of roads to carry lime for soil improvement and tiles to install drainage were factors in dissuading the tenants from cultivating the land. Despite the failures of forestry and arable improvements, the crossbreeding of local cows and shorthorn bulls to produce the Blue-Grey, first shown at the Highland show in 1830, proved a success. What resulted was to become known today as the Galloway: a long-lived hornless cow yielding good quality milk and beef, able to thrive on the hills all year under the protection of its thick, matted coat. A herd book was started in 1877.

The cattle were distinctive and unusual, being kept also on several estates elsewhere in Britain, most famously at Highclere in Hampshire and the Durdans in Surrey. The 2nd Marquess, like other wealthy aristocrats, proud of their special livestock, commissioned a painting from Richard Ansdell, an emerging artist. This shows a brocket faced belted cow with a partially belted calf in a farmyard within a bleak landscape. Entitled "A Galloway Farm", it is presumed to be that exhibited at the Royal Academy in 1840 and still hangs at Dumfries House. In 1843 a tenant of the Butes was delighted with a particular calf born with a white muzzle which he claimed to be the sign of a true Galloway.

John Patrick probably first came to know Old Place in the early 1860s after the death of his mother while he was living with the Earl of Galloway's family at Garlieston nearby. The 12 mile walk or ride over such wild moors combined with his growing religious convictions

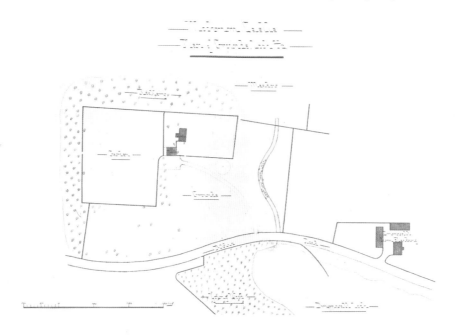

Plan of Mochrum landscape, 1873, by Richard Park.

Richard Ansdell painting, thought to be "A Galloway Farm", exhibited at the Royal Academy in 1840. Note the two Belted Galloway cattle amongst the livestock.

and the closeness to St Ninian's legacy at Whithorn sparked in the young man a deep spiritual connection with the place. Moreover, Mochrum has its own saint, Finbar, who studied under St Ninian. The house, picturesquely set on the edge of Mochrum Loch, had fallen into ruin. Seeing his own property in such a romantic setting but dilapidated condition may have stirred in John Patrick his first desires to conserve and renovate old buildings. The estate, from 1808, had been run as an adjunct to Dumfries House miles away to the north in Ayrshire, and with no resident factor, Old Place had been allowed to settle into its desperate state.

Soon after his marriage, John Patrick asked Richard Park, an obscure local architect, no doubt chosen because his practice was nearby at Newton Stewart, to survey and draw up plans for the restoration of Old Place in March 1873. These show a band of trees to the north and east of the walled orchard named "rookery" and another "young wood" along the west of Mochrum Loch. A stream ran east out of the loch into the Malzie Burn. The restoration of the west tower was nearing completion when John Patrick wrote to his wife in September 1874: "I want to go over to Mochrum again tomorrow, when they promise to have the floors at least partly in... Mochrum is roofed and the outside, barring the slating, is about finished."

Surprisingly there is no distinction deliberately made between the old and new build, which was already being practised by William Burges for the Marquess in Cardiff. Being one of Bute's earlier restoration projects, it predated the Society for the Protection of

Ancient Buildings which William Morris was to found in 1877. This society emphasised the need for honesty in restoration so as not to confuse the viewer with what was original and what was re-constructed. Bute and Park reconstructed the west tower seamlessly. The upper portions were rebuilt too, including the crow-steps of the gables fashioned in the manner quite common in Galloway of small stones and crowned by a larger slab.

John Patrick delighted in staying in the restored west tower, which he described as almost luxurious. He claimed that the fire made the small rooms as warm as a Turkish bath. He used it for the solitude and peace needed for his translation of the Roman breviary, published in 1879. Not everyone shared his enthusiasm for the accommodation, particularly not his biographer Hunter Blair, who described it as a "queer two-storied tower set in the middle of a wild Wigtownshire moor, on the edge of a gloomy lake... here we spent a week together, taking long walks about the country (and a very ugly country it was)

every day, whatever the weather... we lived entirely on trout and grouse." Bute read French novels aloud in the evening for the entertainment of his guests, one of whom became so frenzied by the strange pattern of existence that he implored John Patrick to take him away.

In 1877 Park prepared further plans for the restoration of the second tower and a connecting building using the existing high wall. The Cardiff workshops contributed woodwork and furniture, stone-carving by HG Palliser decorated the renovations and a boat-house was built on the nearby loch. Surprisingly a long period elapsed before its owner returned in July 1889, accompanied by Dimetrios Bikelas whose *Seven Essays on Christian Greece* he had translated and was to publish the following year. By now the roof of the Ladies Tower was completed and the estate interests were in the hands of a new forester and keeper. John Patrick clearly enjoyed the wider landscape, making a point of seeking out a royal fern in flower and showing off ruins of a vitrified fort to his friend.

Watercolour proposal by Robert Weir Schultz for a moat, bridge and gate house at Old Place. Early twentieth century.

Progress at Old Place fell victim to all John Patrick's other projects including Cardiff, Falkland and the rebuilding of Mount Stuart. Park did, however, provide further plans for the fitting out of the Ladies Tower which were completed by the time of Hunter Blair's visit of June 1897. The south garden had already been laid out into its distinctive design with the crazy-paved paths, bordered by grass, enclosing the flower-beds: "a very pretty star shaped garden, gay at this time with crimson ramblers and bright midsummer flowers." The early completion of this garden throws into confusion its authorship since it has been assumed to be by Robert Weir Schultz, but we have no evidence that he had as yet visited Old Place. The pattern of paths depicting two interconnecting crosses, those of St Andrew and St George, and the central paved roundel alluding to that middle feature of a Celtic cross suggest the persistent attachment to religious symbolism in which John Patrick indulged.

The Bute children came in July 1899 and Margaret wrote to her mother: "Here we are safely arrived & quite in love with the place already... We are going to sleep the night in the two lowest rooms of the new part & probably we will keep the new tower & the boys go to the other..." The success of this visit may have persuaded their father to add more comfortable accommodation for his family and he commissioned Park to draw further plans for two ranges to the north and east and enclose the courtyard. Completed after his death in 1902, the buildings were linked by a new archway and outer wooden door to the west tower. The north range, on earlier foundations, housed the kitchen and a baronial hall for dining on the ground floor. A gun-room was later added. The east range accommodated the nursery wing and offices.

It was now that John, the 4th Marquess, employed his first architect Robert Weir Schultz to replace the ageing Park at Old Place. His first task was to embellish the courtyard with cobbles and flagstone paths surrounding a wrought-iron well-head made by his friend, the craftsman Ernest Gimson, at his Pinbury workshop in the Cotswolds. Gimson's partners, Sidney and Ernest Barnsley, made fine Arts and Crafts furniture for the bedrooms, kitchen and dining hall, which complemented those from the Cardiff workshops already in place.

Further building and garden plans which he presented to the family on a visit in 1903 were ambitious. The house was, after all, mostly used in the summer and only occasionally for winter shooting, and good gardening labour was hard to recruit in such an isolated place. He proposed a pergola with 16 stone piers along the east garden wall over a sunken bowling alley and at the south-east corner a small stone garden building with many openings to take in the view. The middle of the star design was to be a stone paved circle surrounded by a hedge, which arched over the eight paths as they ran to meet at the centre. At the south-west corner of the garden was shown a round paved area overlooking a maze outside the wall. Approaching from a two storied stone baronial lodge on the road to the west, an entrance drive was to cross a humped bridge over a new moat, pass stables erected in a new walled yard to the south of the orchard and reach the entrance of the courtyard beside the west tower.

The entire project was scaled down. Only the sundial, inscribed *JCS AD 1905*, signifying John's initials and the date, and a paved viewing area at the south-east corner with a gateway leading to a small garden store underneath were created. The land to the west, where the moat and maze were to have been, was cleared of trees to give a view over Mochrum Loch. Unlike the restoration work on the towers, the division between the old and the new build in the garden was made deliberately obvious. Galloway has a tradition of dry-stone dykes, developed from the eighteenth century, and the gardens were surrounded by fine, partially buttressed, old walls. Different coloured stone with lime mortar was used for any additional capping or the insertion of new gateways through the walls.

The 4th Marquess honeymooned with Augusta Bellingham at Old Place in 1905. A bas-relief carving of the house with birds and trees by Joseph Armitage, now painted white, was fitted over the fireplace in their bedroom to celebrate this occasion. Augusta desired scented flowers in the garden and the beds within the grass-lined paths became filled with summer-flowering shrubs and annuals. The style of living at Mochrum had changed somewhat from the camping conditions of the father to the comfortable abode of the son, who was never accompanied by less than six members of staff. Beside the road was built a pier out into the lake. A dam controlled the outflow of the stream east from the loch from where two separate water pipes fed an innovative electricity generating mill, which may not have been very efficient but nevertheless provided lighting to the house, and a sawmill, each with its own turbine, in a dip below the south garden. Their buildings were designed by Schultz and dated 1903. Loch water pumped up for baths and drinking water drawn from the courtyard well continued in service until mains water was eventually connected 100 years later. In wintertime curling was played on the loch with stones of local granite.

John was also interested in developing the estate for commercial shooting and fishing. This began with planting more trees, particularly oak, ash and birch which he felt were in character with the place, on the flat ground to the west of the estate not suitable for grouse. He specified *Sauch ete,* the Scots for goat willow, to be planted around the edge of the lochs in an attempt to prevent poaching from the shore. The idea was to net for pike regularly on the lochs and stock them with trout from the hatcheries on Bute. The moors

Old Place, 23 September 1937.

The Flower Garden
in 2006.

were to be drained and managed for the development of grouse. In the true tradition of some wealthy landowners he determined to have Galloway cattle, some with white belts, and *Scotch dumpies*, chickens, to intensify the picturesque vision of the moors.

Following the death of a tenant in 1890 and the taking in hand of his cattle, John Patrick had inadvertently founded the Mochrum herd of Galloways, despite his lack of interest. In 1907 the first mention of belted cattle was made at Mochrum and in 1915 two belted cows were bought from another breeder. The society of Belted Galloways with John as one of its founders was established in 1921 and a year later the herd book recorded 200 such animals in 26 herds from all over Britain. When the factor warned that he was spending too much on his farms, John replied: "most people prefer to spend their money on champagne dinners, Mr Hendrie, but I like to spend mine on farms."

Belted cattle are ideal for the moors of the Machars as they are good foragers, eating even purple moor grass, *Molinia caerulea*, in its dense clumps shunned by other stock, and thereby improving the grazing for sheep. Their robustness is fundamental to the management of the landscape around Old Place and helps to retain its moorland characteristics. Sheep were hefted, a technique of management where neither fencing nor intensive shepherding are needed, since it relies on the sheep to train their lambs. The grazing of the two distinct herds of livestock complemented each other.

The house continued as an idyllic summer retreat in August and September for the family of seven children throughout the inter-war period, with its garden showing an exuberance of summer blooms and its orchard, described as an old-fashioned Scottish vegetable garden, producing the needs of the kitchen. During the Second World War the garden paths were turfed over in case their distinctive star design was used by German bombers as a guide towards Glasgow. The garden as a whole, however, was not abandoned like many others during the war and was kept up by Willie Byers, the gardener, who nurtured the beds resplendent with their tall flowers.

In 1947 the estate was settled upon the only one of the sons with a personal interest in farming. Lord David Stuart, who had dropped the appendage Crichton from his surname, moved to Mochrum with his wife and daughters, Flora and Rose, from their country-house

163

on Bute. By the 1970s most of the flower-beds were laid to grass for easier maintenance but the garden's distinctive star pattern was retained. Laburnum and cherry trees, exotic pines, a fine row of elm trees along the road, rhododendrons, azaleas and other flowering shrubs survive from this period. Flora and Rose kept their own gardens and a small arched glasshouse constructed against the south wall of the house. The orchard was used for vegetables but also for many pets, which included Cornwall, the pig, and ornamental sheep. As a child Flora would feed a tame swan from the pier on Mochrum Loch.

David and his brother Robert shot and fished on the estate. During the war, when only reels and not rods were allowed on trains, they would collect bamboo sticks from the beach in order to be able to carry on fishing. There was an annual visit with the gamekeeper to the cormorant breeding site on the nearby islands of Castle Loch. This inland breeding colony, the largest in Britain, has lasted since before 1663 and the birds used to nest along the shore of Mochrum Loch as well as on its islands before abandoning them for the neighbouring loch. The 1790 survey at Old Place records two islands on Castle Loch crowded with birds. By 1911 300 pairs were still breeding in nests made of heather lined with green rushes or sprigs of heather. Management of the colony by ringing birds and removing eggs to limit the population was an important part of the gamekeeper's job, as the birds were known to eat trout, perch and pike as well as sea fish from nearby Luce Bay. Since 1986 250 pairs of cormorants have nested regularly on both lochs as gamekeeping became less intense.

Mochrum Slaethorn by J Mcintosh Patrick, 1958.

Lord David Stuart
on Loch Mochrum,
c. 1950.

David carried on developing his father's herd of Belted Galloway when many of the society's original founders had given up and his animal, Slaethorn, became champion of the Royal and Highland shows in 1955. Many farmers were wary of the markings and actively eliminated the belts from their own herds but the family's almost obsessive devotion to the breeding of 'belties' and their encouragement of others to do so too has undoubtedly saved this fine breed from extinction. Sir Winston Churchill had a small herd at Chartwell in Kent and, when giving up serious farming, retained the herd on sixty acres of fields around the house as an integral part of its landscape. Unfortunately the National Trust underrated their decorative value and sold the cattle when they took over the estate.

In 1964 David transferred the herd to his daughter, Flora, who continued to breed and show, becoming President of the Belted Galloway Society on her father's death in 1973. She imported Canadian bloodlines with which to improve the Mochrum strain and built up a very successful herd of red belted Galloways too. Flora considered the highlight of her life was winning the title of champion of champions for her bull Kestrel at the Wigtownshire agricultural show in 1993. Also keen on rare sheep breeds, she kept, in the orchard, a small flock of Shetlands for their excellent sweet meat and their quality wool which she used to spin. Though Galloways produce good milk, she preferred to drink from Beauty, an Ayrshire house cow, which was milked by Willie Anderson, the shepherd. She rode out everyday on one of her six highland ponies to inspect the cattle while keeping three American quarter horses at the nearby Challoch Glass farm, equipped with its riding ring.

Like her great-grandfather, John Patrick, Flora detested shooting and, though she ate her own farm meat, sold her father's guns and would not allow any within the house. Her

Flora Stuart at
the door into the
courtyard at Old
Place, c. 1960.

gardener and part-time gamekeeper culled foxes and mink but kept her in ignorance of it. She
had a relaxed attitude towards the look of the landscape. The management of the moor, its
appearance and wildlife inevitably changed when shooting stopped with a resultant decrease in
bio-diversity. Increasing numbers of foxes and less intensive heather burning, which encourages
young succulent shoots of heather, led to the decline of red grouse and other game birds,
exacerbated by disease and reduction of habitat by Forestry Commission planting. Moreover,
the trees between the house and the loch grew so tall that its view was lost from the house.

During her stewardship of Old Place, Flora had to contend with a move away
from European subsidies of un-economic hill farming, the outfall from Chernobyl in 1986
which affected south-west Scotland worse than most areas of Britain because of the pattern
of winds, the ravages of BSE, or Mad Cow Disease as it was called, and the Foot and Mouth
outbreak of 2001. All these affected the viability of the estate by threatening sales of the
'belties' from her valuable pedigree herd in markets abroad such as Germany where they
had been fetching very good prices. Advances in breeding practices depended on artificial
insemination and Kingfisher, bred from an Australian bull, was male champion at the Highland
Show for three consecutive years from 1996.

In 1985 the land immediately around the three lochs, Mochrum, Castle and Black,
was designated as a Site of Special Scientific Interest (SSSI) for its *Sphagnum* moss, bog
myrtle *Myrica gale*, and bog rosemary *Andromeda polifolia*, and, its importance as a habitat
for breeding birds was appreciated. Furthermore, in 1995 its European-wide significance was
recognised when it was made a Special Area of Conservation as its active blanket bog was
considered one of the finest examples in the United Kingdom. Salmon, which once may have

spawned in Mochrum Loch, are now being encouraged to come up the Malzie Burn and eels have been seen in the pump house sluice. The special scientific nature of the landscape at Old Place, which John Patrick valued for its many qualities, has now been fully appreciated. A partnership in management has been established with Scottish Natural Heritage.

Flora sadly died in 2004 aged 63 and was buried at the chapel by the shore at Mount Stuart, alongside her family. She left her estate to one of the 4th Marquess' great-grandsons, David Bertie, a farmer, and so Old Place was again passed on to a member of the extended family most suited to its stewardship. His father, Peregrine, remembers holidays there before the war with his own grandfather, the 4th Marquess. A passionate advocate of the pleasures of living off the land, David has introduced a number of changes in the way Old Place is run. Appointing a new local factor, Dougal Evans, David has severed the links with Dumfries House and Mount Stuart which, until then, had provided a management service. Mains water has been connected and the seized-up turbine is being replaced so that power can be generated for the house once again with the intention of paying for itself within eight years.

David has instigated a small pheasant rearing programme to provide for five days of shooting per year. His enjoyment of the sport is matched by his belief that provision for shooting leads to a different approach to land management. The special attention and care of the habitat required for such an activity encourages a richer diversity of wildlife and results in a neater appearance to the landscape. Meanwhile, the outer garden is being enhanced with rhododendrons, supplied by the Stair nursery at nearby Castle Kennedy, the mild and damp climate providing ideal growing conditions.

David Bertie on his estate in Berkshire with his second herd of Belties, 2012.

He has already had experience in keeping 'belties' on his estate in Berkshire with a small herd presented to him by Flora. At Mochrum, he and his farm manager, John McTurk, married to Flora's oldest friend, had success in local shows in 2006 with Lila, one of Flora's last calves, which also became runner-up champion at the Great Yorkshire Show. At the start of this new century David and his young family are using Old Place exactly in the same way that his great-grandfather did in the last and by doing so continues the Bute family's three hundred year connection with Galloway.

St John's Lodge

ST JOHNS LODGE,

THE RESIDENCE OF SIR J. L. GOLDSMID BART.

Tucked away in the centre of Regent's Park, London, is a charming garden, secluded, yet open to the public. It was originally attached to the adjacent St John's Lodge, an elegant cream Regency villa on the inner circle. In 1994 its owners, The Royal Parks, decided to strengthen and enhance its character in the spirit of the 3rd Marquess of Bute's garden, along with a new access walk. This glorious oasis was created from 1892 by Robert Weir Schultz and is very much the tranquil garden of contemplation we see today.

House from the north side of the park in 1844.

The house was part of John Nash's progressive plans to develop the Crown lands of Marylebone Park in 1811 for the Prince Regent. Originally 50 detached villas had been envisaged in a parkland setting but in the end only eight were built. The north end of the park was kept open to protect the rural views of Hampstead and Highgate and eventually opened to the public in 1835. The 18 acres within the inner circle became the Royal Botanical Society gardens. Directly north, across the road from them, St John's Lodge was built by John Raffield in 1818 to a Grecian design for Charles Tulk, MP. The plans were exhibited at the Royal Academy and the house was probably the first to be built in the park. From 1844 it was extended by Charles Barry for Sir Isaac Goldsmid, the banker, into an Italianate palazzo with a ballroom in the *cinquecento* style. An elaborate conservatory 108 foot long with a domed roof was built onto the entire north side of the house. It had both a hardwood and stone floor with large heating pipes from the boiler below. At this time the gardens were informally laid out with lawns and trees.

Previous pages: St John's Lodge from Regent's Park in 2012. The house now sits at the extreme west end of the garden, overlooking the park on the north and west. During the Butes' tenure, this part of the park was incorporated into the garden.

Originally it had been intended that the gardens of the villas would just surround the houses but, in 1836 and 1884, two extra pieces of land were leased by the Goldsmid family, thus increasing the estate to just over 12 acres, with a boundary onto the lake. Sir Julian Goldsmid decided to sell the lease in 1888 and, to maximise his return, sought permission to turn the property into "the national sports club". Fortunately Colonel Kingscote, on behalf of the Crown, decided that this was inappropriate and the lease, along with the two parcels of extra land, was sold on to the 3rd Marquess of Bute as his town house.

From 1881, when in London, John Patrick and his family used to stay at Chiswick House, the cedar-shaded villa of the Duke of Devonshire. He was not keen on the capital and was known to have said "we have no London address, neither of us caring for the place, where no one left me an house and where I have not the least intention of buying one." In a long letter to the editor of the *Scottish Review* he complained about having to leave Mount Stuart to attend a crowded garden party "jammed in a stuffy back garden, in London, in a hollow surrounded by houses, for hours on a midsummer's afternoon."

Chiswick House at this time was unusual as it had escaped the revival of the formal garden, so fashionable in late Victorian times, and resembled the natural idyll which William Robinson, the eminent gardener writer, was so keen on promoting. Contemporary photographs show it as picturesque and overgrown with wonderful specimens of cedars while other trees overhang the lake. Weeping elms and masses of rhododendrons add to the romance. It was, perhaps, these very qualities which had attracted the Marquess. Furthermore his gardener, Mr May, replaced the colourful annual bedding with hardy herbaceous plants, making the whole garden both more sombre and dignified.

However, Chiswick was too distant from the hub of London and, in acquiring the remaining lease on St John's Lodge in 1888, Bute found somewhere in the country and yet only a shilling's cab fare from Piccadilly Circus, a veritable *rus in urbe*. He rapidly set about creating a house and garden for retreat and meditation but which would be suitable for entertainment, particularly now that his daughter, Margaret, was approaching the age when she would be presented at court. He appointed Robert Weir Schultz as architect for the house and garden. Schultz, a Scot, after being articled to Sir Robert Rowand Anderson in Edinburgh was involved with the rebuilding of Mount Stuart, and later moved down to London to work with Richard Norman Shaw.

Schultz won the Royal Academy's gold medal in 1887 for the design of a railway terminus and was awarded a travelling scholarship. He set out to explore Byzantine churches in Greece, Italy and Turkey over the next few years and became involved in drawing and writing about their design. It was his interest in this subject which appealed to the Marquess, who sought a like-minded collaborator in his projects. It may even be that Schultz's interest in the Byzantine had been inspired by the building of St Patrick's Roman Catholic Church in Ayrshire, completed in 1883 to the designs of Anderson and paid for by the Marquess.

Schultz set up his own practice in Grays Inn in 1890 and started to prepare plans for the garden at St John's Lodge the following year, after a meeting with John Patrick in May. Firstly his proposals for planting between the house and road, in January 1892, were

171

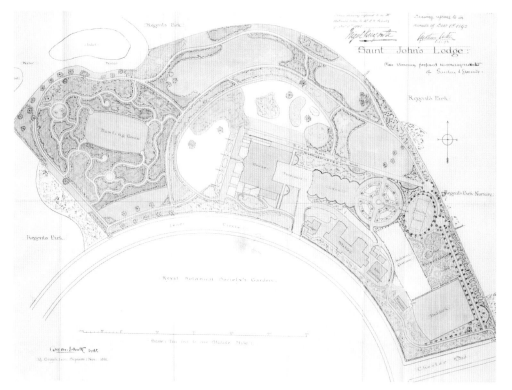

Weir Schultz plan,1892, included part of what is now Regent's Park on the north and west. The chapel was located close to the lake in the north west corner of the plan.

approved by the Crown Estates. Then followed a plan for the whole garden, submitted with an accompanying letter, in November 1892.

> His Lordship proposes to spend a considerable sum of money in rearranging the ground generally & in renewing a large portion of the present shrubs as well as planting largely over the spaces at present laid down to grass. He also proposes a number of new paths as shown on the plan. A comparison of the plan with the ordnance map will at once show the extensive nature of the proposed scheme,

The plans were approved on the 1st December and work began immediately. By February so much had been achieved in the garden that, on writing to his wife, John Patrick seemed delighted: "it is extraordinary how far everything has got on as regards the changes in the grounds. All the rough work seems practically done and appears to me a great improvement. The house is increased in dignity, and the new broad walk appears rather fine."

The design of the garden was not innovative but appeared to make the best of an awkward site. Schultz was clearly influenced by the architect and garden writer, John Dando Sedding, who advocated a gradual merging of garden and landscape, linking art to nature. The early photographs and the fine JJ Joass watercolour exhibited at the Royal Academy in 1897 show how Schultz used the extant mature tree plantings within his scheme, with formality near the house receding into the 'countryside' of Regent's Park. A priest is reported to have said that he could walk on the terrace, with its matchless view of garden and park and forest trees, and often recite his office in perfect quietness, the tumult of London reduced to

JJ Joass aerial perspective, 1897. From the court in front of the house steps descend into the grassed sunken garden. More steps lead up to the circular flower-filled green room, which is connected through the portico to the oval tennis court, backed by the Nymphaeum.

a distant hum and the silence only occasionally broken by the roar of wild beasts in the zoo not far away.

The main axis of the garden, the broad walk, ran east from the house, through a "series of rooms" starting at the forecourt and leading into a sunken lawn bounded with scalloped yew hedges. In each corner of this green theatre stood a stone boy on a tall rusticated pedestal, holding a shield emblazoned with Bute family emblems. It is likely that these pedestals were copied from a pair which had stood in the court and whose use may have been John Patrick's idea since they were uncharacteristic of Schultz's designs. Each end of the lawn had low convex walls covered with ivy and set with wrought iron railings. There were short stone piers along these walls capped by urns filled with trailing ivy. Curved stone steps led down to the grass carpet from gates at each end. The watercolour shows alternate stone statues and benches in the green niches, although it is unlikely that these were ever executed since they do not appear in any photographs.

Column with stone boy holding the Bute emblem, 2006.

St John the Baptist,
c. 1900.

The centrepiece of the garden was a wonderful round flower filled green room, enclosed by another yew hedge and quartered with grass paths. Terms, set into the hedge in the Joass watercolour, appear not to have been executed. In the middle was a stone lined circular basin, filled with water lilies, and symbolically presided over by a statue of St John the Baptist, the Marquess' patron saint. The statue was created by William Goscombe John in polished block tin, otherwise known as pewter. He was the son of Thomas John, a woodcarver employed by the Bute workshops set up in Cardiff for the restoration of its castle. A staircase Thomas had made for the old Mount Stuart, and on which the young William had worked as a trainee with his father, survived the fire of 1877 and was later re-configured for use at St John's Lodge.

Goscombe John trained at the Royal Academy from 1884 and won a travelling scholarship, partly funded by John Patrick, to visit Italy and the Mediterranean. He later won a gold medal from the Academy in 1889 for his group piece "Parting", cast in bronze for Sir Lawrence Alma-Tadema. After a year in Paris studying with Rodin, he returned to London and lived in St John's Wood. Connections to the Marquess through his father and Schultz, who probably knew him as a fellow student, combined with his fine talents made him an obvious choice to design the focus of the garden in 1893. Later versions were cast in bronze, one of which received a gold medal at the Paris Universal Exhibition in 1900.

As approached from the house, the statue was framed by a rather odd-looking stone portico, leading into an oval tennis lawn. The portico, like a Serlian window frame but with squared rather than rounded columns, resembles the window in the red velvet room at Chiswick House, which had been a doorway when John Patrick resided there. This architectural motif sat uneasily in the garden and never really worked as a design feature, and may have

175

been a case where the inexperienced Schultz deferred completely to his patron. With time, however, the hedges and shrubbery grew up so that the portico seemed less awkward. It may even be that the design of the entire broad walk was inspired by Lord Burlington's side garden at Chiswick House. There, a long wide green lawn lined with cedars leads to a semicircular hedge with statues in front, and terms set into the hedge.

The oval tennis lawn appears enclosed on the plan and in the Joass watercolour but it is clear from the ordnance survey maps that the pleached lime hedge, which defined the space, was not fully completed, with the south side remaining open until well into the 1920s. John Patrick's three sons were sent to Harrow school and this area would have been ideal for energetic school boys to relax in on days out. At the other end of the axis from the house was another small circle of pleached limes containing a planted stone urn on a raised plinth and

a stone covered seating area, a miniature nymphaeum, which, like the portico, looked out of balance and clumsy. A formal tree lined walkway led from here back to the house and in the other direction to views out over the park.

Arched seating area, c. 1900.

Beyond the tennis lawn was a rose garden in which Schultz retained a mature poplar tree as the focal point. He designed a robust oak seat to surround its base and an oak gate leading into the vegetable garden beyond, following Sedding's maxim that the garden should become less dressed and acquire its natural 'country' characteristics further away from the house. He placed a rustic dovecote with wooden shingles on an old oak post in one of the rose beds. A small Doric alcove with a tiled floor to the north of the broad walk was erected behind the yew hedge.

Clearly John Patrick revelled in his 'secret' garden while in London. The softness of the mass flower plantings contrasting with the formal yew lined rooms, set off by mature trees leading away into the distant park, achieved that balance of solitude and peace that he needed. Regent's Park engaged him in other ways too. He belonged to both the botanical and zoological societies whose gardens were located there and on Sunday afternoons would delight in walking through both with guests or family, often talking freely with the keepers who knew him well.

To the west of the house was a terrace on which sat a sundial, now lost. The formal bowling green, designed by Schultz to occupy the land beyond, was never carried out, perhaps because the Butes preferred a more rural setting. This area of the garden, overlooking the lake to the north, was left informal, with its mature elms disguising the different levels leading down to the lake. A simple field, therefore, separated the terrace from the lake and this was to become the site of the sunken chapel.

Nymphaeum, c. 1900.

In 1892 a request was submitted to the Crown Estates to build a small chapel within the house. *Truth* magazine reported that this was rejected for fear of depreciating the value of the property. Clearly John Patrick's religion was still causing waves within society. The article, however, was based on a misunderstanding. The request of the lessee was soon accommodated and the chapel was completed within the house. By 1899 it was clearly insufficient for the family's needs and Schultz was commissioned to submit further plans, beautifully drawn, for a sunken Byzantine style chapel near the lake. To overcome possible objections by both the Crown estates and the public it was agreed that the chapel would be well surrounded by shrubs and removed on the expiration of the lease. The tiny building, at a cost of £996, was quite bizarre, half buried in the ground and, when completed a year later,

was clearly visible from both the inner circle and the park, though quickly camouflaged as the shrubs grew higher and thicker. It took on greater significance as its patron died soon after without probably ever having seen it finished.

Tree seat and dovecote, c. 1900.

John Patrick intended that all his houses would be installed with electricity, being convinced that it was a lasting and worthwhile invention when others were still sceptical. Schultz was commissioned to design lighting for both the house and the garden at St John's Lodge, and, in 1894, was experimenting with lighting up the statue of St John the Baptist as well as the rest of the garden. No doubt this was a highlight for guests as they looked out of the ballroom, lit with garlands of Venetian glass, on to the illuminated grounds.

The entire garden was surrounded by oak pales and, in 1899, its gates were replaced with oak farm gates to match in, hung on oak piers to replace the existing "cement" [sic] ones, giving the property an even more rural quality. The Crown Estates' manager commented that they appeared rather wide but matched those that were already there. He stipulated that they open inwards and only one gate be used for normal occasions but both for receptions. By 1911 these pales were becoming too expensive to repair and the Crown had begun to replace them with iron railings. The dowager Marchioness became very agitated by this and insisted that the Crown stop work to the boundary. After two years she appeared to have won her way and it was even commented that the lodge's paling looked better than the cheap new railings surrounding The Holme, an adjacent villa.

The lease was due to expire in 1916 and for the last five years complicated negotiations were conducted, initially with the dowager Marchioness and later with the 4th Marquess. At stake was the extra amount of land within the garden, which they had been leasing. By August 1912 the Marquess agreed to give up some land to the east and south, which adjoined the Crown estates nurseries, and asked his solicitors, Farrers, to conclude the deal. However, in the meantime, there were questions raised in parliament and articles in *The Times* suggesting that the public needed more land in Regent's Park, particularly greater access to the lake. The sunken chapel proved the stumbling block in the negotiations. There seemed to be no way that it could be included within the curtilage of the house and kept separate from the park and the public, even though the Marquess agreed to a path alongside the lake. In the end the Marquess found another house and the lease with 6.75 acres of land was put up for sale in July 1916.

In the last few months before the end of the lease the pewter statue of St John was presented to a convent in north London, from where it was later moved to Cardiff Castle. It is now in the grounds of the late Sir Julian Hodge's house in Lisvane, a suburb of Cardiff. The Thomas John staircase was removed and put in the attic of Mount Stuart and a new staircase was approved and fitted. Finally the chapel in the field was demolished, the hole re-filled and the surface re-turfed. The dowager Marchioness wrote to her son, Lord Colum, on 23 June: "we have just had the last Mass in the Chapel in the field, this being the nativity of St John. It is really very sad all these last events."

Just at the point when the house was to be re-leased, in 1916, the Crown Estates decided to lease it for free to the Red Cross as a hospital for the duration of the war. 5.5 acres of garden were returned to the park, mostly on the west and north sides, and re-fenced with iron railings, but the oak paling was left along the inner circle. An arrangement was made for the gardens to be maintained by the Royal Botanical Society from across the road at its own expense. Miss Packer of Queen Elizabeth's School, Kensington put on an amateur performance of a *Midsummer Nights Dream* on 22 July for the benefit of St Dunstan's Blind Soldiers and Sailors Hostel. This performance in the Butes' green theatre set within Regent's Park was a foretaste for today's popular "Shakespeare in the park".

Later that year William Cutbush of Highgate Nurseries was commissioned to carry out drastic surgery to about 50 trees at St John's lodge for a cost of £127. A large elm and a large chestnut tree on the lawns had their lower branches removed and two large black poplars were pollarded. The heads of limes along the broad walk and the side-walk were also cut back and some trees, which were dead or dying, were removed completely. The following year the pollarded black poplars looked so terrible that they were taken out along with some old elms along inner circle, which were leaning dangerously over the road. The need for so much tree work suggests that the Butes preferred a balance between nature and art, a less manicured arboreal canopy contrasting with lawns, hedges and flowers beds maintained to a very high standard. At

The statue of Hylas and the Nymph replaced that of *St John the Baptist* in the pond in the centre of the garden, 2007.

the end of the war the Marquess, who appears to have removed the stone boys with their shields from the piers when he left, offered them back to the garden, where they remain standing today.

In 1920 the National Institute for the Blind leased the property on behalf of St Dunstan's which needed a permanent headquarters away from traffic. The rose garden and kitchen gardens were built over with single-storied workshops, yet all was not lost. Herbaceous borders were planted in front of the scalloped hedge and the pleached lime hedge was completed around the oval tennis lawn to block out the view of the workshops. This space was made into an azalea garden.

In 1928 a Cabinet decision was made that enclosures within the royal parks should be given back to the parks when their leases expired. This coincided with St Dunstan's decision that it no longer required such a large building as the lodge but would find the temporary buildings in the kitchen garden sufficient for its needs. Captain Ian Fraser MP, their chairman, who had himself lost his sight in the war, persuaded the Crown that a conversion of the stables into a bungalow for himself should be exchanged for the lease of the house and much of the grounds. Schultz's broad walk, the lily pond and the oval tennis lawn were opened to the public, thus considerably reducing the garden area around the house.

The statue of Hylas and the Nymph by Henry Pegram, now in the middle of the lily pond, was presented to the garden by the Royal Academy, to fill the gap created by the removal of St John the Baptist. A few years later, in 1934, the portico and nymphaeum were dismantled. This stimulated a number of angry letters to *The Times*, including one from Goscombe John, living nearby, who complained about "this unnecessary act of vandalism".

The house, part of London University for over 50 years, is now privately leased by the Sultan of Brunei. What was left of the public gardens was renovated in 1994 by Simon Hoare of Colvin and Moggridge. A new entrance was made to the south of the garage block to allow the house more privacy. The scalloped hedge, which had been replanted with privet, was again grubbed up and planted with yew. Gradually the pleached limes are being renewed. In response to a public consultation, the 1920s herbaceous borders beside the scalloped hedge were retained and new wooden benches commissioned. A metal arbour was erected where the portico had been and a small arched seat was added in the oval lawn near the site of the nymphaeum. Since so much land had been lost to the original garden, it was impossible to recreate anything more than the broad walk vista and part of the side-walk back to the house. It is still a garden of contemplation and quietness with a plaque at the gate crediting its concept and origin to John Patrick.

Looking towards the metal arbour which replaced the stone portico, now covered in creepers to give it a more solid appearance. Wisteria time, 2010.

Bibliography

Adam, Robert, *The Works of Robert and James Adam, Esquires, Number III, Containing part of the designs of Luton House in Bedfordshire, one of the Seats of the Earl of Bute*, London: Author, 1775.

Adams, Ian H, *Papers on Peter May Land Surveyor 1749–1793*, Edinburgh: Printed for the Scottish History Society by T&A Constable, 1979.

Andrews, Henry, *The Botanists Repository for New and Rare Plants*, London: Author, 1797.

Austen, William, *This History of Luton with its Hamlets*, Newport, Isle of Wight: County Press, 1855.

Backer, CA, *Verklarend Woordenboek Van Wetenschappelijke Plantennamen*, Groningen: Noorhoof, 1936.

Baxter, EV & Rintoul LJ, *The Birds of Scotland*, Edinburgh, London: Oliver & Boyd, 1953.

Blair, David Oswald Hunter, *A Medley of Memoirs*, Edinburgh, London: Oliver & Boyd, 1953.

Blair, David Oswald Hunter, *John Patrick Third Marquess of Bute KT (1847–1900) A Memoir*, London: John Murray, 1921.

Blair, David Oswald Hunter, *A Last Medley of Memoirs*, London: E Arnold & Co, 1936.

Campbell-Culver, Maggie, *The Origins of Plants*, London: Headline, 2001.

Cane, Percy, *The Creative Art of Garden Design*, London: Country Life, 1967.

Cane, Percy, *The Earth is My Canvas*, London: E Arnold & Co, 1936.

Cardiff City Council, *Bute Park Restoration and Development Plan*, Cardiff: Cardiff City Council, 2005.

Cardiff County Council, *Arboretum Tree List*, Cardiff: Cardiff City Council, 1995.

Clutton Brock, Juliet, and Stephen JG Hall, *Two Hundred Years of British Farm Livestock*, London: HMSO, Natural History Museum 1995, c. 1989.

Chambers, William, *Plans, Elevations and Perspective Views at Kew*, London: William Chambers, 1763.

Davies, John, *Cardiff and the Marquesses of Bute*, Cardiff: University of Wales Press on behalf of the History and Law Committee of the Board of Celtic Studies, 1981.

Davis, Frederick, *Luton, Past & Present: Its History and Antiquities*, Luton: W Stalker, 1874.

Desmond, Ray, *Kew, The History of the Royal Botanic Gardens*, London: Harvill with the Royal Botanic Gardens, Kew, 1998.

Donnachie, Ian L and Innes MacLeod, *Old Galloway*, Newton Abbot: David and Charles, 1974.

Drummond, Maldwin, ed, John Bute, *An Informal Portrait*, Wilby: Michael Russell, 1996.

Elliot, Brent, *Victorian Gardens*, London: Batsford, 1990.

Fleming, John, *Robert Adam and his Circle, in Edinburgh and Rome*, London: John Murray, 1962.

Franklin, Robert, *Lord Stuart de Rothesay*, Brighton: Book Guild, 2008.

Franklin, Robert, *The Stuarts of Highcliffe*, Christchurch, Dorset: Natula Publications, 1998.

Fraser, Flora, *Princesses, The Six Daughters of George III*, London: John Murray, 2004.

Gardner, Martin, et al, *Threatened Plants of Central and South Chile*, Edinburgh: Royal Botanic Gardens Edinburgh, 2006.

Gifford, John, *William Adam 1689–1748: a life and times of Scotland's universal architect*, Edinburgh: Mainstream, 1989.

Gilpin, William, *Remarks on Forestry Scenery*, London: R Blamire, 1791.

Groom, Susanne, & Prosser, Lee, *Kew Palace*, London: Merrell, 2006.

Hannah, Rosemary, *Alive to Kindness*, Durham: University of Durham, 2000.

Hare, Augustus, *The Story of Two Noble Lives, Being memorials of Charlotte, Countess Canning, and Louisa, Marchioness of Waterford LP*, London: George Allen, 1893.

Harris, John, *Sir William Chambers, Knight of the Polar Star*, London: Zwemmer, 1970.

Harrison, Christina, *Heritage Trees in an Historic Landscape—MA Garden History Thesis*, London: Birkbeck College, 2004.

Hassell, J, *Tour of the Isle of Wight*, London: T Hookham, 1790.

Hayden, Ruth, *Mrs Delany, her Life and her Flowers*, London: British Museum, 2000.

Hedley, Olwen, *Queen Charlotte*, London: John Murray, 1975.

Henrey, Blanche, *No Ordinary Gardener Thomas Knowlton, 1691–1781*, London: British Museum (Natural History), 1986.

Herringshaw, Sheila, *A Portrait of Highcliffe*, Christchurch: Natula Publications, 2004.

Hetherington, Paul, *Byzantine and Medieval Greece*, London: John Murray, 1991.

King, David, *Complete Works of John & Robert Adam*, Oxford: Architectural Press, 2001.

Laird, Mark, *The Flowering of the English Landscape, 1720–1800*, Philadelphia: University of Pennsylvania Press, 1999.

Mason Neale, Rev. John, *A History of the Holy Eastern Church* London: 1850.

Mathew, Manjil, *The History of the Royal Botanic Garden Library Edinburgh*, Edinburgh: HMSO, 1986.

Mawson, Thomas, *The Life & Work of An English Landscape Architect*, London: Richards Press, 1927.

Mawson, Thomas, *The Art and Craft of Garden Making*, London: Batsford, 1907.

McLees, David, *Castell Coch*, Cardiff: Cadw, 2005.

McIlroy, Pamela, *A History of the Falkland Estate*, Falkland: Falkland Conservation Group, 2004.

McIntosh,Charles, *The new and improved practical gardener, and modern horticulturist*, London: T Kelly, 1852.

McKerlie, PH, *Lands & Their Owners in Galloway*, Edinburgh: W Paterson, 1877.

McWilliam, John, *The Birds of the Island of Bute*, London: HF & G Witherby, 1927.

Morgan, Dennis, *The Cardiff Story*, Cowbridge: D Brown and Sons, 2001.

Mowl, Timothy, *Historic Gardens of Dorset*, Stroud: Tempus, 2003.

Ottewill, David, *The Edwardian Garden*, London: Yale University Press, 1989.

Paterson, James, *History of the County of Ayr: with a genealogical account of the families of Ayrshire*, Ayr: J Dick, 1847.

Pettigrew, Andrew, *The Public Parks and Recreation Grounds of Cardiff, Vol. 1*. Compiled by AA Pettigrew, Roath Park, Cardiff 1926, reviewed 1933–1934. Unpublished manuscript. Cardiff Public Library.

Phibbs, John, *Luton Hoo, Bedfordshire, A History of the Landscape: for Elite Hotels, Luton*, Luton: Central Bedfordshire Council Planning Department, 2003.

Pullar, Polly, *Rural Portraits: Scottish native farm animals, characters and landscapes*, Wigtown: Langford Press, 2003.

Renn, Derek, *Caerphilly Castle*, Cardiff: Cadw, 2002.

Rix, Martyn, *The Art of the Botanist*, Guildford: Lutterworth, 1981.

Roberts, Jane, ed., *George III & Queen Charlotte, Patronage, Collecting and Court Taste*, London: Royal Collections Publications, 2004.

Roxburgh, William, *Plants of the Coast of Coromandel Published under the direction of Sir Joseph Banks*, London: 1795.

Rousseau, GS ed., *Letters and Papers of Sir John Hill 1714–1775*, New York: AMS Press, 1982.

Rykwert, Joseph and Anne Rykwert, *The Brothers Adam: The Men and the Style*, London: Collins, 1985.

Russell, Francis, *John, 3rd Earl of Bute, Patron & Collector*, London: Merrion Press, 2004.

Scottish Natural Heritage, *An Inventory of Gardens and Designed Landscapes*, Edinburgh: Historic Scotland, 1987 and 2006.

Schweizer, Karl ed., *Lord Bute, Essays in Re-interpretation*, Leicester: University of Leicester Press, 1988.

Smith John, *Treatise on the Management and Cultivation of Forest Trees*, Glasgow: 1843.

Smith, Sir James Edward, *A Selection of the Correspondence of Linnaeus, and other Naturalists from the Original Manuscripts*, London: Longman, 1821.

Skinner and Dyke, *A Catalogue of the Great Part of the Capital Mansion house, Offices, Conservatory and Temples... Highcliffe Mansion House*, London: 1795.

Stamp, Gavin, *Robert Weir Schultz, Architect, and his work for the Marquess of Bute*, London: Curwen Press, 1981.

Steven, Helen, *The Cumnocks Old and New*, 1899.

Strawhorn, John, *The New History of Cumnock*, Cumnock: RD Hunter for Cumnock Council, 1966.

Stroud, Dorothy, *Capability Brown*, London: Faber, 1975.

Stuart, Lord David, *An Illustrated History of Belted Cattle*, Edinburgh: Scottish Academic Press, 2006.

Stuart Wortley, *The Hon Mrs E, Highcliffe & the Stuarts*, London: John Murray, 1927.

Stuart Wortley, *The Hon Mrs E, A Prime Minister and his Son*, London: John Murrary, 1925.

Thomas, Hilary M, *The Diaries of John Bird of Cardiff, Clerk to the 1st Marquess of Bute 1790–1803*, Cardiff: South Wales Record Society and Glamorgan Archive Service, 1987.

Tyhurst, Frank, *The Coast of Highcliffe Castle*, Christchurch: Natula Publications, 2003.

Verney, Peter, *The Gardens of Scotland*, London: Batsford, 1976.

Verey, Rosemary, *Garden Plans*, London: Frances Lincoln, 1993.

Vivian, Frances, *A Life of Frederick, Prince of Wales, 1707–1751*, Lampeter: Edwin Mellen Press, 2007.

Warner, Richard, *A Companion in a Tour Round Lymington*, Southampton: 1789.

Warrick, John, *History of Old Cumnock*, Paisley: Alexander Gardener, 1899.

Waterford, Louisa, *Memoirs*, Privately printed in various versions: no date.

Webb, Fiona, *Highcliffe Castle Management Plan*. London: Architectural Association thesis, 2000.

Williams, Matthew, *Cardiff Castle*, Cardiff: Scala, 2008.

Wilson, EJ, *James Lee and the Vineyard Nursery Hammersmith*, London: Hammersmith Local History Group.

Manuscripts & Articles

Bute MSS at Mount Stuart, Isle of Bute.

Stevenson Collection of Highcliffe archives.

The Statistical Accounts of Scotland 1794–1845, online resource, 1996.

Dingwall, Christopher, "Walled Kitchen Gardens in Scotland—an historical overview", *National Trust for Scotland Head Gardeners Meeting, The Cromarty Centre*, 16 September 2004.

Falkland Heritage Trust "House of Falkland: Information notes for walkers exploring the historic landscape", 2002.

Garnier, Richard, "Alexander Roos (c. 1810–1881)" *The Georgian Group Journal*, vol. XV, 2006, pp. 11–61.

Gardner, Martin F, and Philip Thomas, "The Conifer conservation programme", *The New Plantsman*, vol. 3, part 1, 1996, pp. 5–21.

Gardner, Martin F, "The conservation potential of a Chilean conifer and a climber", *The New Plantsman*, vol. 7, part 3, 2000. pp. 174–177.

Gilbert, Christopher, "Thomas Chippendale at Dumfries House", *Burlington Magazine* vol. 111, no. 800, Nov 1969, pp. 633–677.

Sanderson, Margaret, "Robert Adam in Ayrshire", *Ayrshire Monographs*, no. 11, 1993.

Shields, Steffie, "'Mr Brown Engineer': Lancelot Brown's Early Work at Grimsthorpe Castle and Stowe", *Garden History*, vol. 34, no. 2, 2006, pp. 174–191.

Symes, Michael, "The Plantings at Whitton", *Garden History*, vol. 14, no. 2, 1986, pp. 138–172.

Waterford, Louisa, "Recollections to the Age of 12", *Highcliffe Parish Magazine*, 1891.

Country Life, articles on the individual properties.

The Walpole Society, "The Vertue Notebooks", vol. 18, 1929–1930.

The Walpole Society, "The Vertue Notebooks", vol. 30, 1951–1952.

Transactions of the Buteshire Natural History Society, vol. IV, 1910–1911, pp. 25–45.

Transactions of the Scottish Arboricultural Society, vol. 9, 1879, pp. 73–81.

Acknowledgements

Particular thanks to The Marquess of Bute, and to former Archivist at Mount Stuart, Andrew McLean, both of whom have generously spent considerable time and effort helping us with this book.

Others who have also given their time, expertise and patience to help us are:

John Adair
Willie Anderson
Graham Alcorn
James Alexander-Sinclair
Vince Bell
Suzanne Benfield
David Bertie
Peregrine Bertie
Richard Biffen
Julia Buckley
Chris Bull
The Dowager Marchioness of Bute
Susan Campbell
David Caselton
Adrian Cook
Derek Cooper
Tommy Cooper
Anthony Crichton Stuart
Marietta Crichton Stuart
Ninian Crichton Stuart
Sophie Crichton Stuart
Christopher Dingwall
Tommy Donnelly
Elite Hotels Ltd
Sheila and Richard Evans
Brent Elliott
Gina Fullerlove
Martin Gardner
David Gemmell
Bill Girvan
Jan Haenraets
Rosemary Hannah

Christina Harrison
Adam Higgins
Rosie James
James Kay
Sarah Kellam
Oonagh Kennedy
Ann Mathewson
David McCracken
Catriona and Henry MacDermot
Pam McIlroy
Charles McKean
John and Monica McTurk
Nick Mellish
Maria Miller
Lynsey Nairn
David Ottewill
The Earl Peel
Fiona Peel
John Phibbs
George Ramsay
Miguel de Riglos
Francis Russell
Billy Shields
Steffie Shields
Tony Shorey
Edith and Robert Stevenson
Ian Stevenson
Michael Symes
Nigel Taylor
Frank Tyhurst
The Lord Weir
Matthew Williams

Credits

Picture Credits

Index

Colophon

© 2012 Artifice books on architecture and the authors.
All rights reserved.

Artifice books on architecture
10A Acton Street
London
WC1X 9NG

t. +44 (0)207 713 5097
f. +44 (0)207 713 8682
sales@artificebooksonline.com
www.artificebooksonline.com

All opinions expressed within this publication are those of
the authors and not necessarily of the publisher.

Designed by Mónica Oliveira at Artifice books on architecture.
Edited at Artifice books on architecture.

Cover image
Detail: Painting of the walled garden with view to Dumfries
House by Jacob Thomson, 1830. Image courtesy of Mount
Stuart Trust.

Frontispiece
Stewartia malacodendron, collage by Mrs Delany, July 1778.
Linneaus named the plant and its genus for 3rd Earl of Bute
in 1742, although by that time his surname had changed its
spelling to Stuart.

British Library Cataloguing-in-Publication Data.
A CIP record for this book is available from the British Library.

ISBN 978 1 908967 02 2

All rights reserved. No part of this publication may be
reproduced, stored in a retrieval system, or transmitted,
in any form or by any means, electronic, mechanical,
photocopying, recording, or otherwise, without prior
permission of the publisher.

Every effort has been made to trace the copyright holders,
but if any have been inadvertently overlooked the necessary
arrangements will be made at the first opportunity.

Artifice books on architecture is an environmentally responsible
company. *Passion, Plants and Patronage* is printed on FSC
accredited paper.

The Paul Mellon
Centre for Studies in
British Art.